How to Pray Well

Other books by Raoul Plus
from Sophia Institute Press®:

Holy Simplicity
How to Pray Always
Progress in Divine Union

Raoul Plus, S.J.

How to Pray Well

SOPHIA INSTITUTE PRESS®
Manchester, New Hampshire

This English translation from the French of *How to Pray Well* was originally published by Burns, Oates, and Washbourne Ltd., London, in 1929. This 2009 edition by Sophia Institute Press® includes minor editorial revisions.

Sophia Institute Press®
Box 5284, Manchester, NH 03108
1-800-888-9344
www.sophiainstitute.com

Nihil obstat: John V. Simcox, *Censor deputatus*
Imprimatur: Edm. Can. Surmont, *Vicarius generalis*
Westmonasterii, May 9, 1929

Library of Congress Cataloging-in-Publication Data

Plus, Raoul, 1882-1958.
    [Comment bien prier. English]
    How to pray well / Raoul Plus.
        p. cm.
    Originally published: London : Burns, Oates & Washbourne, 1929. With minor editorial revisions.
    Includes bibliographical references.
    ISBN 978-1-933184-55-5 (pbk. : alk. paper) 1. Prayer — Christianity. I. Title.
    BV215.P5413 2009
    248.3′2 — dc22

                                        2009017533

09 10 11 12 13 14 10 9 8 7 6 5 4 3 2 1

Contents

Book One
The Prayer of Adoration

Book Two
The Prayer of Thanksgiving

❧

How to Pray Well

Editor's note: The biblical quotations in the following pages are taken from the Douay-Rheims edition of the Old and New Testaments. Where applicable, quotations have been cross-referenced with the differing names and enumeration in the Revised Standard Version, using the following symbol: (RSV =).

Book One

The Prayer of Adoration

Chapter One

❧

The Most Perfect Prayer

We may pray to adore, to give thanks, to implore pardon, or to ask for the graces we need. But whereas, in the last three cases, our thought comes back to ourselves, in the first, we forget ourselves entirely and think of God alone.

If I give thanks, it is because I have received; if I implore pardon, it is because I have sinned; if I ask, it is because I need. *I* am never absent from my prayer. But in the prayer of adoration, the only person considered is God, to whom I pray. There is no intrusion of the creature. He who prays is not mentioned; he disappears utterly. He does not think of himself; he counts for nothing: "We praise Thee, O Lord; we adore Thee, O Lord; we bless Thee, O Lord; Glory be to God on high; O Lord, we sing Thy glory."

I do not suggest that this is the only kind of prayer that we must offer. It will be seen later that the prayer of thanksgiving, the prayer for pardon, and the prayer of petition are excellent, legitimate and, by reason of our very condition as creatures, quite necessary. But I say that this kind of prayer is in itself the most perfect; it is the prayer that gives greatest glory to God, that in which we most truly fulfill our duty as creatures, since thereby we unreservedly devote the whole of ourselves to singing the praises of our Creator. Moreover, by this prayer we most truly fulfill our function as intelligent and loving creatures, since the canticle of praise that ascends from our hearts shows that we appreciate what God is in Himself, and how much He deserves that we should venerate and adore Him.

Some, in view of the excellence of the prayer of adoration, have contended that prayers which involve the element of self (thanksgiving, prayer for pardon, petition) are to be excluded. They reason in this way: pure love is the best; hence, we must keep only pure love, and any spiritual act in which self enters, however secondarily and imperceptibly, is to be regarded as an evil love and almost a sin.

This is a spirituality which ignores the facts of human nature. Pascal used to say that if you try to make man an angel, you make him an ass. We are not angels, but frail creatures of flesh and blood. We are not yet dwellers in the land where the eternal *Sanctus* resounds; and if we give a thought to things other than God, we are not doing wrong. It is not wrong to make known our wants, to ask for mercy, and to give thanks for blessings received. On the contrary, this is precisely what a creature might normally be expected to do when he is in need, when he has sinned, when he has been loaded with benefits.

This being made quite clear, it still remains true that many Christians, even good Christians, do not make sufficient use of the prayer of adoration. We instinctively ask God for favors and implore pardon for our sins; but there is a regrettable tendency to forget praise and adoration. It is not wrong, it is even advisable and necessary, to think of ourselves. But sometimes, at least, we might think of God only. The Quietists were wrong to say that we must always do this; but we may try to do it occasionally, because such prayer is the most perfect practice of the Christian religion.

It is conceivable that someone, without excluding other forms of prayer as being evil, may rightly decide that he will not use them himself, but devote his attention for long periods or even habitually to the prayer of adoration. After being for a long time in close touch with God, he loses the desire to ask anything for himself. His petition is all for God. In the Our Father he willingly pauses in the middle: "Thy kingdom come, Thy will be done . . . hallowed be Thy name." In the rest: "give us . . . forgive us . . . deliver us," he has little or no further interest. He knows that God is good, merciful, infinite; that is enough for him. What need is there for him to speak to God of himself? To God he prefers to speak of God.

How to Pray Well

It is permissible to go even further. Toward the end of his *Spiritual Exercises*, St. Ignatius[1] suggests to the retreatant "the contemplation for divine love," and in this contemplation, first of all, thanksgiving to God for His benefits. But he advises going beyond this. God is not only what he is *for you*; he is what he is *in Himself*. He is Creator, Providence, Giver of all blessings; but before all He is God. Put aside all other thoughts, and concentrate upon this ultimate fact, this final consideration. Love God not for what He gives to us; love God for what He gives to Himself eternally, for that unceasing intercommunication between the Father and the Son, for the eternal act whereby the Father contemplates Himself, for the reciprocal love between the Father and the Son, the result of which is the eternal procession of the Person of the Holy Spirit. *O beata Trinitas*, O Blessed Trinity!

Be it noted, however, that we have called this the ultimate fact, the final consideration. To want *everyone* to have pure love and to use only the prayer of adoration is a dream, and a heretical dream at that. But it is quite another thing, when a person has reached the stage at which he has wholly decided upon perfect generosity and the complete

---

[1] St. Ignatius of Loyola (1491-1556), founder of the Jesuit Order and author of the *Spiritual Exercises*.

offering of himself to God, to advise him to practice pure love, complete forgetfulness of self, and definitively, as far as is possible on this earth, to make "his conversation in heaven" — that is, to live entirely in God.

To sum up: The prayer of adoration is very perfect, the most perfect of all, in itself. Hence, it is advisable to practice acts of it occasionally. From this, however, it must not be concluded that the other forms of prayer are to be condemned, and that we are not to give thanks or to ask pardon or benefits of God. It is an error to hold that the *state* of pure love is possible for all or, in an exclusive sense, desirable for everyone. But what we may conclude is that it is not surprising to find in a generous soul a strong inclination to place the prayer of praise and adoration in the forefront of the spiritual life, and that, moreover, it is desirable for Christians in general occasionally to leave the everlasting prayer of petition and to rise sometimes, and even often — as the Church invites us — to the disinterested prayer of praise.

To help these souls we will indicate the two forms that the prayer of adoration may take: affective adoration, which consists in *transports* of the heart, and effective adoration, which finds expression in acts, in faithful, loving and devoted *service*.

Chapter Two

ᑲᐟᐤ

Affective Adoration

꿈

Affective adoration manifests itself in words and aspirations. St. Francis of Assisi had just received from our Lord the signal favor of the stigmata. When he came out of his ecstasy, he wrote the following "Praises":

Thou art holy, O Lord God, who alone workest wonders. Thou art great. Thou art all-high. Thou art the Almighty King, the Holy Father, the King of heaven and earth. Thou art the Lord, three in one, the universal God. Thou art the Good, the supreme Good, the Lord God, true and living. Thou art Charity and Love. Thou art Wisdom. Thou art Humility. Thou art Patience. Thou art Security. Thou art Repose. Thou art Joy and Happiness . . .[2]

Every day before the canonical hours and before the office of the Blessed Virgin, the saint, glowing with love, counseled this prayer:

[2] St. Francis of Assisi (1182-1226), founder of the Franciscan Order.

How to Pray Well

O Sovereign God, most holy and most high, supreme good, universal good, absolute good, who alone art good, we offer Thee all praise, all glory, all thanksgiving, all honor, all benediction, and we praise Thee unceasingly for all things that are.

Similarly, reciting the office of the Passion composed by himself, he finishes with these words:

Let us bless the Lord God, living and true: praise, glory, honor, and benediction; let us ever render to Him all good. *Amen, amen. Fiat, fiat.*

The Prayers of St. Mechtilde and St. Gertrude also contain beautiful examples of this type of prayer. St. Mechtilde[3] prays as follows:

O Lord, Thou art eternal Wisdom who knowest all things in heaven and on earth. Thou alone knowest Thyself perfectly and fully; no creature can comprehend Thee. O God, Thou art immense and incomprehensible in Thy omnipotence. All the beings of heaven and earth together would not avail to praise Thee enough. Thou alone art capable of giving to

---

[3] St. Mechtilde of Helfta (c. 1241-1298), nun, visionary, and mystic.

Thyself full praise; Thou alone knowest fully with what abundance of love Thou givest Thyself to the soul that loves Thee. I praise thee, O Lord, with all my strength, with all my Senses, with all my movements. I praise Thee in Thyself and for Thyself, cleaving to Thee, and I desire that all in heaven and on earth may become partakers of Thy grace, O my God.

St. Mechtilde asked our Lord one day: "Most sweet and loving Lord, how wouldst Thou have me spend my time?"

Jesus answered her, "In giving praise."

"Very well," replied the nun, "teach me, so that I may be able to praise Thee worthily."

The Master thereupon taught her a wonderful litany of praise.[4]

In the monastery of Helfta in Saxony, Mechtilde, who had been put in charge of the instruction of the oblates, received in the year 1261 a young girl who was later to be the great Gertrude.[5] Doubtless she — and still more, the Holy Spirit — taught her how to pray. God is not merely a benefactor to whom we go with requests, a sort of supreme

---

[4] *Revelations of St. Mechtilde*, Bk. 2, ch. 35.

[5] St. Gertrude (1256-1302), Benedictine nun, visionary, and mystic.

infirmarian to whom we go for remedies whenever we are in need; He is above all the sovereign Majesty and, as St. Ignatius always says when he mentions God, "our Lord and our God."

Gertrude habitually used to praise the three divine Persons in these words:

O ever adorable Trinity, I exalt Thy immense and generous goodness, while I consider all the graces which from the depths of Thy abyss are so abundantly bestowed upon the Blessed.

I praise Thee, secondly, for all the graces which Thou hast granted to the most holy Mother of God.

I praise Thee also for all the grace which Thou hast poured forth upon the sacred humanity of Jesus Christ.

Glory to Thee, O sovereign, most excellent, most glorious, most noble, most sweet, most gracious, glorious and ever tranquil and ineffable Trinity, Godhead and Unity before all ages and now and forever!

I praise Thee, O ever adorable Trinity. I would that it were possible in the hour of my last agony to sing Thy praises so devotedly as therein to spend my last strength, that I might lose my life in praising Thee, O my God.

This cult of adoration for the sovereign Majesty of God did not in any way diminish her familiarity or restrain her tenderness. That this is so may be seen from the delightful little book of P. Cros *The Heart of St. Gertrude*, where he condenses the best of the famous work *The Herald of Divine Love*. It was the Jansenists who later placed too exclusive an emphasis upon certain of God's attributes to the practical neglect of others, and thus gave rise to that repellent piety whose chief characteristics were fear and austerity, and from which modern spirituality, in spite of the efforts of our Savior to reveal to us the mercies of His divine Heart, has not yet succeeded in freeing itself completely.

The Jesuit Nieremberg is known especially as the author of the beautiful book *The Price of Grace*. To show that the affective prayer of adoration is common to all schools of piety, I quote the following powerful passage. It is entitled "Joy of the soul by reason of the Divine Immensity":

It is a great joy to me, O my God, to know that Thou art immense; for, since Thou art everywhere, I am sure always to be able to find Thee. What a supreme happiness! Wherever I may be, He who is the love of my soul, my friend, my beloved, my King, my Father, my Spouse, my sovereign Good, in a word, my God, sees me always, hears me, and sustains me. What happiness not to have to take even a step in order to be where my God and my Love is! I rejoice, O my God, in what makes my joy and Thy glory — namely, that in no place art Thou absent, and that everywhere Thou art present. How afflicted should I be, O my God, if Thou were far from me! With what earnestness would I go in search of Thee, were Thou a million leagues distant from me!

But finding Thee so near to me, how happy I am! I rejoice, I am filled with content and gladness when I consider what makes for my happiness and for Thy glory. Thou art near me to help me, by my side to hear me, within me to sustain me and to load me with a thousand blessings. How couldst Thou help hearing me, when I ask that which Thou desirest to give me? And Thy presence near to me does not hinder Thy presence elsewhere; for thou art whole and entire everywhere; nay, space itself cannot contain Thee; Thy greatness extends beyond the sun and the moon, beyond the firmament, it rises above the heavens, to the ends of the world. Where, then, my Beloved, could I go and not meet Thee, since even in those places which I can never reach Thou art ever present?

How precious in the eyes of them that love
Thee is this attribute of immensity, how useful for
them that fear Thee! He who loves Thee will find
Thee everywhere; him that feareth Thee, everywhere Thou shalt find. How, then, can the sinner
fly from Thee, who canst find him wherever he may
fly? If he descend into the bowels of the earth, God
is there, if he rise above the stars, there he will meet
his Judge; if he cross the seas, he cannot escape his
Creator; if he fly into the air, he will find Him upon
the wings of the wind.

No sinner can separate himself from Thee; Thou
canst not separate Thyself from him who serves
Thee. Make me fear Thee, make me love Thee,
make me serve Thee, make me rejoice in Thy company in the glory of my heavenly home, since even
in this land of exile Thou art not far from me.

Nearer our own time is Elizabeth of the Trinity, the Carmelite of Dijon and spiritual sister of Thérèse of Lisieux;[6]
so different from her and yet so like. Her favorite prayer is

---

[6] Bl. Elizabeth of the Trinity (1880-1906), Carmelite
nun known for her great mystical writings; St. Thérèse
of Lisieux (1873-1897), Carmelite nun famous for her
"little way" of spirituality.

well known: "O my God, Trinity that I adore." It will become more well known, thanks to the commentary upon it written by Dom Vandeur in a little book that takes its title from the first words of the prayer. Elizabeth desired nothing else than to be a "victim of praise." She wished to be "simply an adorer"; and in this aspiration many have followed her.

Yet, beautiful as these prayers and transports are, they do not approach the glorious spirit of adoration found in some of the canticles of the Bible and in the Psalms. Here, and especially in the Psalms, we find the most wonderful flowers of praise. We will not quote from them, since the reader has easy access to them in his prayer-book or his missal. Let him read especially the Psalm *Laudate pueri*,[7] from the Vespers of Sunday, the *Laudate Dominum omnes gentes*,[8] from the Vespers for Feast-days, and the *Ecce nunc benedicite Dominum*[9] from Compline. We may well understand why the Church has called the recitation of the office an "uninterrupted praise," *laus perennis*, and anyone desiring to foster the spirit of adoration and praise would do well to make the office the subject of his meditations.

[7] Ps. 112 (RSV = Ps. 113).
[8] Ps. 116 (RSV = Ps. 117).
[9] Luke 1:68-79.

Let us imitate the Church and her liturgy in her zeal for praise. It is said that St. Teresa[10] almost fainted when she heard the words in the *Credo* at Mass: *Cuius regni non erit finis* — "of whose kingdom there shall be no end" — so filled was she with zeal for the honor of God. Let us learn to love and to adore like the saints, and when God takes us from this life, let our last words be those of St. Thomas Aquinas,[11] from the *Te Deum: Tu Rex gloriae, Christe!* Thou, O Christ, art the King of Glory."

---

[10] St. Teresa of Avila (1515-1582), Spanish Carmelite nun and mystic.

[11] St. Thomas Aquinas (c. 1225-1274), Dominican philosopher and theologian.

Chapter Three

∽

Effective Adoration

Transports of adoration are excellent, but service is better. It is well to say that you love, but to *show* that you love, to show it by your acts, and if necessary by heroic acts, this is the triumph of perfect adoration.

Of all creatures, the most Christlike is Mary. None better than she has ever practiced effective and affective adoration simultaneously. Since her example far surpasses that of any of the saints, we must dwell a while upon it.

Filled to overflowing with the love of God, the silent Virgin — for the Gospel relates but few of her words — one day gives expression to the praise that is in her heart. From that day forth, anyone who wishes to find a song that best exalts the glory of God on earth will find it in the triumphant *Magnificat* the Virgin recited at the age of sixteen when she visited her cousin Elizabeth. She seems to say: "My soul would like, if it could, to make God even greater than he is. I thirst for an ever-more-radiant glory for Him whom I love, who is the Almighty, *Magnificat anima mea Dominum . . . qui potens est.*"[12]

But still more moving than this ecstasy of affective adoration is the proof that our Blessed Lady gave to the Most High of her *effective* adoration.

God decreed the Incarnation. As Faber says in his poetic way:

> Innumerable decrees of God, decrees without number, like the waves of the sea, decrees that included or gave forth all other decrees, came up to the midnight room at Nazareth, as it were to the feet of that most wonderful of God's creatures, with the resistless momentum which had been given them from eternity, all glistening with the manifold splendors of the divine perfection, like huge billows just curling to break upon the shore; and they stayed themselves there, halted in full course, and hung their accomplishment upon the Maiden's word.[13]

God, who needs not to have recourse to man's freewill, deigns to subordinate the accomplishment of His divine decrees to the will of a daughter of men, to the

[12] Luke 1:46 ff.
[13] *Bethlehem*, 74.

consent of this tender virgin of the race of David, who lived during the reign of Augustus in the obscure village of Nazareth.

In the beginning, it was a woman who, by abusing her freewill, lost supernatural grace for the whole of mankind. It was a woman who — at what price we shall now tell — submitted her will to God by a moving act of heroism, and thus paved the way for the restoration of grace. The Word of God, the Wisdom of the Father, that He may come into the world to save the world, deigns to ask the consent of His creature. On Mary's consent all will depend. If she consents, we are saved. If she refuses, how shall the redemption be accomplished?

It was an awful moment. It was fully in Mary's power to have refused. Impossible as the consequences seem to make it, the matter was with her, and never did free creature exercise its freedom more freely than she did that night. How the angels must have hung over that moment! With what adorable delight and unspeakable complacency did not the Holy Trinity await the opening of her lips, the *fiat* of her whom God had evoked out of nothingness, and whose own *fiat* was now to be music in His ears, creation's echo to that *fiat* of His at whose irresistible sweetness creation itself sprang into being! Earth only, poor, stupid, unconscious earth slept in its cold moonshine.

We may foresee what Mary's answer will be. Who is it that speaks to her? Who is it that, while He might demand, yet stoops to beg her consent through the Angel Gabriel? It is God. As soon as she is certain that this is no lying voice, that the messenger is no phantom of her imagination, that the proposal made to her is no illusion; when she has seen behind the form of the Angel who speaks to her the invisible image of the Most High, then, since her chief desire is to serve, to serve to the utmost of her power, she bows her head — for to receive the Angel, she, the Queen of Angels, had remained standing while her messenger and servant knelt at her feet — and then herself falling upon her knees accepts the will of God: *Fiat . . . ecce ancilla.* "Be it done unto me according to thy word. Behold the handmaid of the Lord." The handmaid is one who serves. The Most High may count upon me; I am His.

There had not been yet on earth, nor in the angels' world, an act of adoration so nearly worthy of God as that consent of hers, that conformity of her deep lowliness to the magnificent and transforming will of God.[14]

Nor is it to be thought that this acceptance of the divine decree on Mary's part was to cost her nothing. To become Mother of the Redeemer meant to accept the conditions of the Redemption. It would be her task to prepare her divine Son for the hard wood of the Cross. Our Lord said that he who loves is ready to give his life for his beloved. Mary, that she might "serve" in the fullest sense of the word, would give her life. She would give up the life of her Son, she would give up her own. Calvary would be the scene of a twofold martyrdom: that of the mother and that of the Son.

An even more perfect model of effective adoration than Mary is our blessed Lord Himself.

As the Word dwelling eternally in the brightness of heaven, the Son of God could not adore. To adore, one must be an inferior. But the three persons of the Blessed Trinity are equal; none is superior, none is inferior. The Son equal in all things to the Father may love the Father; He cannot adore Him.

[14] *Bethlehem*, 74.

Desiring to give to his Father a divinely conceived form of love, the Word decreed to become man. Equal to the Father, He will become inferior to Him, not as God, but as man; and thus, He will be able to adore Him. In heaven He cannot adore; on earth He can.

Some theologians[15] hold the attractive view that even had Adam not sinned, the Word would still have become man. Of the two ends of the Incarnation — the glorification of the Father and the salvation of mankind — the former would have been sufficient, and according to some, *was* sufficient, to induce the Word to become a son of men. Christ is the one object of the divine complaisance, and the motive for which the Word came upon earth was the adoration that he wished to give to His Father. The expiation of sin was but secondary in the divine plan.

However this may be, even if we admit with the majority of theologians that both ends were the cause of the Incarnation, it remains true that the desire to procure the glory of His Father by an act of adoration of infinite value loomed large in the plans of the Savior.

By coming upon earth, the Word loses none of His sovereign majesty. He becomes less than the Father, but

[15] John Duns Scotus (1266-1308) and many of the Franciscan school.

He remains the Infinite. Less than the Father, He can adore Him; infinite, He can adore Him infinitely. Since the Word became man, there is on this little earth of ours one who is capable of giving to the infinite God an infinite adoration: the Word of God made flesh.

In words of extreme delicacy and yet of rare power Fr. Faber, whom we have already quoted in connection with Mary — his favorite subject — clearly emphasizes the adoring power that was in Jesus from the first moment of His conception. After recalling the glory given to God by Mary's consent, Fr. Faber adds:

But another moment and there will be an act of adoration greater far than that. Now God is free. Mary has made Him free. The creature has added fresh liberty to the Creator. She has unchained the decrees, and made the sign, and in their procession, like mountainous waves of light, they broke over her in floods of golden splendor. The eternal Sea laved the queenly creature all around, and the divine complacency rolled above her in majestic peals of soft mysterious thunder, and a God-like Shadow falls upon her for a moment, and Gabriel had disappeared, and without shock, or sound, or so much as a tingling stillness, God in a created nature sate in His immensity within her bosom, and the eternal will was done, and creation was complete. Far off a storm of jubilee swept far-flashing through the angelic world. But the Mother heard not, heeded not. Her head sank upon her bosom, and her soul lay down in a silence which was like the peace of God. The word was made Flesh.[16]

And later, dealing more fully with this unprecedented act of adoration, he writes:

It was a finite act, and yet of value infinite. Then first was the blessed majesty of God worshiped as it deserved to be . . . with a worship equal to Himself. . . That first act of love is not ended yet. It has stretched from that old midnight at Nazareth to this hour, and is not weakened by the stretch.

The existence which began that night in Mary's bosom . . . was first of all, a life of oblation. Worship was its predominant idea. Adoration was the mold in which it was cast.[17]

---

[16] *Bethlehem*, 75.
[17] Ibid., 76, 97, 98-99.

Chapter Four

Adoration through Christ and in Christ

All Christians know that God became man for us. Not all, however, realize that He did more than this. Not only did He become one of us; He willed also to make each one of us a part of Himself. In addition to the mystery of the Incarnation, there is the mystery of Incorporation. We are incorporated into the person of Christ.

Christ might have been content to pay for us, as it were, "from without," like one who, hearing that his neighbor is in debt, says to him, "I will pay for you. How much do you want? Here is the money." This would be generosity, but it would not create a bond of blood between the two; such a gift would not make them children of the same Father. They become greater friends; they do not become relatives.

Many imagine that our Lord is nothing more than a very generous divine neighbor. We could not pay the debt; He put at our disposition a great fortune: His manger, His Cross, every moment of His life, every drop of His blood; and by this means God was satisfied and forgave us our debt.

Had our redemption been accomplished in this way, it would still have been a priceless favor. But our Savior has done incomparably more than this. Not only has He put Himself in our place; He has identified Himself with us. He has not been content to remain an outsider — however divinely generous — He has made us His brethren, children of the same Father. He has engrafted us on His own person. In the operation of grafting, the bark and the sapwood are pierced, and grooves are made through which the sap may flow and give life to the branch engrafted. So it was with Christ. He, the living vine, was placed upon the hard wood of the Cross and in His hands, His feet, and His side were made deep wounds, and through the merit of those wounds, the divine life, which is in Him in all its fullness, passed from Him into us. Henceforth we are branches grafted upon Him, called to live His life.

When Christ appears before his Father, He is not alone, but we are with Him. Without us He is not completely Himself. Not physically, indeed, but mystically, we are a part of Him. The full and complete Christ is at once one and manifold. The complete Christ is Jesus, the Son of the Father, the son of Mary, together with all of us who are become divine through and in Jesus Christ.

We have recalled these details of the doctrine of our incorporation in Christ, although we have studied them more fully elsewhere, first, because they cannot be too much emphasized, and secondly, because they will throw light upon what still remains to be said.

The result of the Incarnation was that one who is truly God is capable of giving adoration and, precisely because he is God, of giving infinite adoration. Thanks to our incorporation in Christ, this mystery becomes more wonderful still. Only one person in the world, we said, can glorify God as He deserves — namely, Christ Jesus. But by the mystery of incorporation, through Baptism we become an integral part of Christ, and every increase of sanctifying grace makes us more a part of Christ than before. In this manner, the whole of the adoring power of Christ is placed at our disposal.

As an integral part of the mystical body of Christ — *plenarium corpus Christi*, as St Augustine[18] puts it — I benefit by the advantages of this sublime union. Only Christ can give to God a glory that is worthy of God; but of this Christ I am a part. I am nothing, if I consider myself as a creature enclosed in my own solitary personality with all my deficiencies, and hence, I am quite incapable of giving to God any but an insignificant worship . . . Since I am a creature, I am obviously bound to give to Him all the

[18] St. Augustine (354-430), Bishop of Hippo.

glory that He expects from me; but what glory is that? What can an infinitesimal atom give to its maker; what homage can a bit of debased metal from the divine workshop offer to the Most High?

Gaze one fine evening at the myriads of stars scattered through space, and think what this earth of ours is, in comparison with all these worlds. The most recently discovered have taken three thousand years to send us their light, and their weight in pounds would be expressed in thirty or forty figures. Charts of the heavens already show 140,000 stars, and each one of these, like our sun, is the center of a similar system! In the midst of all these worlds, what is this little earth of ours, and on this earth of ours, what is a mere man? A mere atom, a mere nothing. And this nothing talks of adoring God! Yet adore he must, for it is his duty as a creature. But can he adore? Can he give a worship that is worthwhile? He can, and in a way that is undoubtedly worthwhile. This he can do because he is not merely a man; he is a "Christ."

This insignificant earth of ours — and a rebellious earth at that — was chosen by the Word for his Incarnation. But He did more; He willed to go to the very extreme in His love for us. The inhabitants of this earth had been raised at the beginning to a divine dignity; but from that high estate they had fallen, and were dead. God willed to raise them to the dignity of being "other Christs." He, Christ, will be the head; human beings, supernaturalized by the grace that his merits have restored to us, will be His members. And when Christ appears before His Father with the words "Behold your beloved Son, in whom you are well pleased," He will include us in His oblation.

The complete Christ is made up of the head and the members together. Hence, when, being in the state of grace, we offer up prayer of adoration to the Father through and in Jesus Christ, our worship will not be merely the worship of a creature, but a worship to which the Son of God adds all that it needs in order to give condign glory to the Father. In fact, our Lord asks us to be His *complement,* to make up, with St. Paul, what is wanting to the sufferings of Christ.[19]

But He, our Savior, the head of the Mystical Body, the divine head of all deified souls, constitutes our divine *supplement.* He supplies, in the fullest sense of the word, all that is lacking in our offering. This was human; He makes it divine, He makes it a "Christ-prayer" and therefore a prayer worthy of God. The model prayer, the most excellent of all prayers — whether it be the prayer of worship, of thanksgiving, of contrition, or of petition — is the offering that we make to God of His Son, Jesus Christ.

[19] Col. 1:24.

How to Pray Well

Elsewhere we have pointed out that by Baptism we are given part in a priesthood — not indeed a complete, but yet a spiritual and a royal priesthood — whereby we are able privately — not officially or publicly — to offer Christ to his Father. When the Church prays, she prays in this way, gathering into the prayer of Christ all the poor prayers of us members of his Body; poor prayers indeed, yet endowed with a divine, a salutary, and a glorious character, because they are offered "in Christ."

The culmination of this joint prayer, of this prayer truly worthy of God, is the Mass, in which Christ again offers His supreme Sacrifice. Our Lord's supreme act of worship was His death on the Cross. There did our Savior recognize most completely the sovereign majesty of God, when He submitted to the will of the Most High, even to the yielding of His life. Having assumed the nothingness of our human nature, He willed to submit to the lot of mankind; He died. Every Mass renews this recognition on the part of Christ of God's sovereign rights; and hence, every Mass represents the apex of adoration.

This reflection should help us when we assist at Mass; it should help us whenever we pray. In answer to the invitation of the priest at Mass: *Orate fratres*, we pray, "May the Lord receive this sacrifice from thy hands, to the praise and glory of His name, to our benefit and to that of all His holy Church." So also the *Imitation of Christ* bids us offer ourselves during Mass in this way: "Lord, in the simplicity of my heart I offer myself to Thee this day, as Thy servant forevermore, for Thy homage and for a sacrifice of perpetual praise. Receive me with this sacred oblation of Thy Precious Body, which I offer to Thee this day in the invisible presence of assisting angels, that it may be for salvation unto me and all Thy people."[20]

"Since, O my divine Brother," writes St. Gertrude, "Thou didst become man to make reparation for all the faults of mankind, I beseech Thee to intercede for me with Thy Blessed Mother, and make up on my behalf for all that has been wanting in the praises that I have addressed to her."[21] So also St. Mechtilde: "Glory be to Thee, most sweet, most noble, most glorious Trinity, ever tranquil and ineffable. Deign, O Lord, to join the words *most sweet* to Thy divine sweetness; the words *most noble* to Thy excellent nobility; the word *resplendent* to Thy inaccessible light; the word *tranquil* to Thy peaceful repose; the word *ineffable* to Thy unspeakable goodness."

May our prayer of adoration rise to these heights. This is a truly Christian prayer.

---

[20] Thomas à Kempis, *Imitation of Christ*, Bk. 1, ch. 9.

[21] *Revelations of St. Gertrude*.

Book Two

The Prayer of Thanksgiving

Chapter Five

∞

The Rarity of Gratitude

∞

A Sinhalese sharpshooter during the war made this curious reflection: "If a Frenchman is in distress, it is always 'My God, my God, help me!' If he is happy, it is 'God! I care nothing for God!' "

The statement is a cruel generalization. Yet all must admit that the truth contained in this criticism is applicable to many prayers in all parts of the world. In need we ask God for help; but when God has answered, how many there are who forget to give thanks. Few prayers were ever more sincere than those of the ten lepers in the Gospel. What cries and laments! "Jesus, son of David, have mercy on us."[22] The Master comes and heals them, and immediately off they go, proclaiming their joy everywhere, without a thought of thanks for their benefactor. Only one — ten percent is the usual proportion of gratitude that is found between man and man or between man and God! — only one, who has previously been led away by the

[22] Luke 17:13.

others, thinks of returning to the Divine Healer. "There were ten made whole. And where are the nine?"[23]

Consider how great is the goodness of our Divine Master, who, knowing man's habitual ingratitude, yet willed to devote Himself as He has done to man's salvation. Nevertheless on certain occasions He has shown how pained He is by man's ungrateful attitude. "What afflicts me most," he said to Margaret Mary,[24] "is this lack of gratitude." That the wicked should sin one can understand; but it is hard that the good should be ungrateful. "Good" people are terrible at times. If they only realized how thoughtless they can be!

And why is gratitude so rare? Because man's heart is so narrow. Once he has a thing, he never reflects that he has received it, that everything he possesses comes from another, from him who possesses all things. He lives entirely in the present, forgetting the moment in which he was in need. Now that he is rich, he forgets the past. Although man is endowed with the faculty of memory, he seems

[23] Luke 17:17.

[24] St. Margaret Mary Alacoque (1647-1690), Visitation nun who received revelations of and promoted devotion to the Sacred Heart of Jesus.

constitutionally incapable of remembering his debts of gratitude. The following scene, described by a shrewd observer, is quite typical. John, five years old, had a little sister Pauline, who had fallen ill. For several evenings, his mother made him add to his prayers, "O God, make Pauline better." The following week, the special invocation was suppressed.

"Why," asked John, "don't we pray for Pauline now?"

"Because God has made her better, darling."

"Then why don't we thank Him?"

In man's present state, if he is in distress, he cries for help; if he is happy, he rejoices. If there were no sorrow in the world, there would be little prayer. It is a shameful confession to have to make, but it is true. To ask, we need only to think of ourselves; to give thanks, we have to think of another. For asking, we need only self-interest; for thanksgiving, we need love. If there were as many *ex-voto* offerings as there were prayers answered, one house out of every two would be a church or a chapel, and then even the walls would not suffice to hold them all. But we are not likely to have to face that difficulty; thank-offerings are not in proportion to petitions. And even when there is gratitude, it is not very lasting.

The winter of the year 1784 was, apparently, a very severe one. Louis XVI commanded fires to be lighted in the barracks, hospitals, and homes for the poor, and he himself made tours of inspection, to see that his orders had been carried out, and to give alms. At the end of the winter, the people in their gratitude put up a monument to him near the Louvre, made of snow! And these were the same "good people" who were soon to invade the palace of Versailles.

History does not change. Among those who so fiercely cried, "Away with Him, crucify Him" on Good Friday, I am sure there were some who had sung an enthusiastic *Alleluia* on Palm Sunday. There is not much gratitude to be found among men, and even what there is does not last for long.

If only ingratitude were a sin of "wicked" people. But it is not. Of its nature it is a sin of "good" people. Our Lord indicates this when He commends the leper who had been cleansed for coming to render thanks: "Of the ten, none is come to give thanks save this stranger."[25] Ingratitude is the sin of friends and acquaintances. St. John brings this home to us when, in speaking of the coming of our Lord upon earth, and of the cold reception accorded Him, he says, "He came unto His own, and His own received Him not."[26] St Paul, who knew that the giving of thanks, which

[25] Luke 17:18.
[26] John 1:2.

ought naturally to follow benefits received, is far from being spontaneous, insists on this duty lest we forget it. "Give thanks always for all things," he writes to the Ephesians, "in the name of our Lord Jesus Christ to God and the Father."[27] Similarly he reminds the Corinthians, the Philippians, the Colossians, and Timothy of the great duty of gratitude to God for benefits received.[28]

This insistence is significant. The Curé d'Ars[29] marveled that while there were so many orders and institutes for the purpose of adoration and reparation, there were none for thanksgiving. Since his time, the lacuna has been filled; but it is curious that we should have had to wait so long.[30]

[27] Eph. 5:20.

[28] 2 Cor. 9:2; Phil. 4:6; Col. 2:7, 4:2; 1 Tim. 4:3.

[29] Curé d'Ars: St. John Vianney (1786-1859), patron saint of parish priests.

[30] The "Institute of Thanksgiving" was founded at Mauron (Morbihan) by a nun of the "Reparatrice," superior of the convent at Lyons, who felt herself irresistibly drawn to thanksgiving rather than to reparation. By the advice of her directors, she left the congregation of Rue d'Ulm to found, under the name of Marie of the Blessed Sacrament, first the Congregation of Thanksgiving for the laity in 1857, and later the Community of Thanksgiving, for the special object of giving thanks for the institution of the Blessed Sacrament. We may also

How to Pray Well

Even if grateful souls are rare, even if there are not many for whom it is a spontaneous impulse to give thanks, yet they do exist. There are some whose only desire is to devote their whole lives to thanksgiving.

The Blessed Pierre Lefèvre, one of the first companions of St. Ignatius, lived in the constant practice of thanksgiving. Thanksgiving was his very life; he thanked God for everything. He thanked Him for the glory that He had given to the angels and the saints. Knowing how little gratitude man showed to God, he constituted himself a sort of purveyor of thanksgiving to the Most High, and used to thank Him for all the graces that He had been pleased to give even to the least and the most hidden among men. Whenever he saw good fortune or success anywhere, he offered thanks to God for it, in case the fortunate recipient should have forgotten to do so. As he passed through town and country, he praised God for all the beautiful things with which the earth was blessed. He gave thanks for the sins and the neglect that God's grace had enabled him to avoid; he thanked God for the graces that God would have given to him had he corresponded more faithfully.

> mention the Sisters of Thanksgiving at Castelnaudary, and the Sisters of the Annunciation at Joinville and Langres, whose object is to give thanks for the great blessing of the Incarnation.

Another well-known Jesuit, P. Louis du Pont, in the preface to his *Meditations*, recommends thanking God for the gifts he has granted to those who, through their own fault, are damned and will therefore never have the opportunity of thanking God for all that His providence has done for them.

A good man of our acquaintance had the original habit of thanking God for favors at the time of asking them. Was not this the advice that our Lord himself gave to St. Gertrude: to give thanks beforehand for graces not yet received?

But the prototype of thanksgiving to which we must always return is our Lady. Her *Magnificat*, which is a song of praise and adoration, is also a sublime hymn of thanksgiving. "He that is mighty hath done great things to me. Can I do otherwise than rejoice in blessing the Most High who is my salvation?"

There are some who imagine that humility consists in denying or forgetting the gifts of God. True humility, after the model of Mary, consists in recognizing favors received, but remembering that they are favors — that is, something we do not possess of ourselves, but which we have only from God's bounty.

Gratitude shows itself under its most meritorious guise in time of affliction and suffering. One *Deo gratias* in time of adversity, according to John of Avila,[31] is worth six thousand in time of prosperity. It needs a great faith in God, a supreme recognition of the rights of the Most High, of His mercy and His goodness, to see the reality beyond appearances; beyond the visible hand that wounds to discern the invisible heart that loves and allows the wound only to give an opportunity of courage and increase in love. When St. Chantal[32] learned that her son had been killed in war, she said, "O my God, I thank Thee for the honor that Thou hast done me in taking my only son while he was engaged in fighting for the Church of Rome." Her husband, mortally wounded in the hunt, said to the man who had killed him by his negligence, "This shot came from heaven before it left your hand"; and to his wife, "Let us give praise to divine providence; let us look at this blow in its heavenly source."

More recently, but no less heroically, Consummata,[33] hearing that one of her brothers, an aviator during the war, had fallen in enemy territory from an altitude of 2,000 meters, his airplane in flames, said to the Prioress of

---

[31] St. John of Avila (d. 1569), Spanish secular priest, writer, and missionary in Andalusia.

[32] St. Jane Frances de Chantal (1572-1641), foundress of the Visitation Order.

[33] Marie-Antoinette de Geuser.

Carmel, "My parents are very grieved, of course, but they are very brave. Will you help me to thank God, who gives them His strengthening grace; and especially will you give thanks with me for the fulfillment of the adorable will of our great God of Love?"[34]

Do the lives of the saints contain a more admirable prayer? Earlier, in the month of November 1914, the brave child, hearing of the first war-losses and of the death of many members of her own family, added the following postscript to one of her letters: "Let us give thanks ever for all things. What a joy it is to suffer to the full, to give all!" Uniting effective thanksgiving to her prayers, she added, "We must give thanks not only in word, as St. John says, but in deed and truth. It is not enough to say, 'My soul, bless the Lord'; we must add, 'And let all that is within me glorify His holy Name!'[35] 'Thank you' is indeed the fruit of a grateful love; but it is not the complete fruit. The crown of love is our correspondence with grace, the adapting of every fiber of our being to the least of God's desires. This continual state of love, united with joy and gratitude, is what I call true thanksgiving; and my dream

[34] Unpublished letter of October 22, 1916. In her biography, it is clear that thanksgiving has a great part in the life of this crucified and ever-joyful soul.

[35] Cf. Ps. 102:1 (RSV = Ps. 103:1).

would be to raise up legions of souls with such faith, confidence, and love and that their gratitude to God would make of them living thank-offerings, wholly consecrated to His glory."

We know, in a country that is not France, one who may be called a sister to Consummata, by reason of her terrible physical sufferings — she has been two years in bed suffering from abscess — and by reason of her joy in the midst of pain. She writes — and all her letters are in similar strain — "Bless God with me, because I am too happy, too overwhelmed with favors." How true it is that as a soul devotes herself more and more to God, so does God show more and more generosity toward her. Such a soul experiences Calvary and Tabor at the same time, but Tabor rather than Calvary. Having a further abscess in her right hand that prevents her even from writing her usual penciled lines, she contrives to scribble as follows: "I have some difficulty in writing; but with the help of our Lord, I do what I can. I am sure you will understand."

To be sure, I understand. May God give more souls that know how to thank Him, souls that can forget themselves so far as to give thanks even in time of suffering, souls truly devoted to thanksgiving.

We need hardly say that, as with the prayer of adoration, so also with the prayer of thanksgiving, the only thanksgiving worthy of God is that of our Lord Jesus Christ; and the moment when this thanksgiving reaches its highest perfection is in the Sacrifice of the Mass. Does not the word *Eucharist* mean "thanksgiving"? Especially during the last few years, there has been a great increase of devotion to the sacrament of the Eucharist. But there is not the same degree of what one may call the *spirit* of the Eucharist. By the spirit of the Eucharist, I mean the spirit of gratitude, homage, and thanksgiving to God. Just as the Eucharist is the essential part, and one may say the center of Catholic worship, so the spirit of the Eucharist ought to be the predominant element in our prayers. As a matter of fact, it is usually the least prominent.

After all, we are not destitute; we are laden with benefits — in a moment we will describe them in detail. What we have received is incomparably more important than what we lack. Surely, then, thanks ought to come before petitions. If we but realized better that we are of God's own family, we should not behave so much like beggars; we should more often give our hearts to God instead of stretching forth our hands. We only know how to beg; let us try and love a little. And the best way to love is to recognize what love our Father in heaven has shown in granting us so many favors. Let us not forget what we have already said many times before, that petition is not the whole of prayer, nor even is it the chief part. In heaven we shall pray — in fact, we shall do nothing else; and our prayer will no longer be one of petition. There will be no need to ask for anything, for we shall be filled with glory to the capacity we have attained through our life of grace. All will be thanksgiving, love, and adoration.

Let us use a little more on earth the prayer that we shall use exclusively in heaven.

Chapter Six

∽

Gratitude for the Blessings of Nature

There are four great works of God by which we benefit. They are Creation, the Incarnation, grace, and glory. The last two we shall treat as one, for they are but two aspects of the one gift.

We will deal first with the gift of Creation, without which all the others would be vain. Although Creation occupies so important a place in theology and in apologetics, yet, generally speaking, it seems to have little interest for spiritual writers. This is a great pity. They seem to prefer those points of doctrine which depend upon God's revelation rather than upon natural philosophy alone, and especially they insist upon those in which God shows His great goodness. Creation reveals to us above all things the greatness of God.

St. Ignatius is one of those who has best shown how meditation upon divine creation may be used to spiritual advantage. To arouse sentiments of love — for the greatness of God, properly understood, does not terrify; it attracts — the great spiritual teacher bids the retreatant who wishes to achieve disinterested service to consider: how God gives; how he renders Himself present to all that He gives; and how He puts something of His own, and how He works, in all that He gives.

∞

How generous God has been in dispensing His benefits! Just as He has crowded space with myriads of worlds, so He has multiplied on the earth the various species — over a hundred thousand — of flowers, insects, and precious stones.

And what wonderful harmony do we not discern therein, whether we consider them as a whole or one by one. When a body passes from the liquid to the solid state, its molecules arrange themselves side by side to form a geometrical figure, which is always exactly the same. When a plant reproduces itself, it passes through the same stages of development without fail, and how fascinating it is to watch these cellular developments under the microscope! It is a delightful display of arabesques and artistic curves. We know an artist who devoted himself exclusively to this branch of biology, simply to enjoy the splendors revealed by the microscope. Why is it that the sea contains so much salt that, if it were all collected, it would foam a mountain higher than Mont Blanc? Think what would happen otherwise to all the refuse that is carried into the sea from the rivers. Would it not become a plague spot for the human race? Like rivers as they flow through town and country, so the blood that circulates in our body collects poison in transit, which it then discharges into the lungs. But this must be done quickly, or asphyxia will supervene; and that is why the lungs, although enclosed within so small a space, have a surface area of two hundred square meters!

These are but a few examples among a thousand that we might consider; but they help us to understand how Bossuet could exclaim, "It was indeed a bountiful and splendid alms that Thou gavest, O God, when Thou didst create the world." No wonder that St. Francis of Assisi wrote his "Canticle of Creatures," or that the Franciscan convert St. Serafino of Montegranaro,[36] when reproached with taking delight in the perfume of roses, answered, "Merely to look at them moves me to the depths of my heart." Crispin of Viterbo,[37] another Franciscan, was so delighted with the spectacle of creation that he kept repeating, "How beautiful the world is!"

[36] St. Serafino of Montegranaro (d. 1604), Capuchin known for his simplicity, obedience, and asceticism.

[37] St. Crispin of Viterbo (1668-1750), Francisan lay-brother known for his simplicity and humility.

How to Pray Well

Admiration of nature is not confined to saints. Victor Hugo protested that the thought of the wonders of nature drew him to prayer in spite of himself. Then there was Marc Boasson, the young artist whose letters written during the war contain sublime hymns of thanksgiving. In June 1916, after contemplating the sunset he said, "Thank God for eyes to see it and for a soul to feel it!" Another time, filled with admiration at the sight of nature coming to life again: "How thankful I am to God for having let me see the spring once more!"

Was it Dupuytren or Ricamier who, after an anatomical experiment, invited his pupils to kneel down and thank God for the wonders of creation? When, in the year 1869, a committee was formed to erect a statue to Morse during his lifetime, the great inventor of telegraphy asked that on the bronze scroll that was to be put in the hand of the statue should be written the words: "It is the work of God"; and on the occasion of the inauguration of telegraphy, the message that he had broadcast to the whole world ended with the words: "Glory be to God in the highest, and on earth peace to men of goodwill."

Fabre, the famous entomologist, sometimes breaks off in the middle of his description of insects to sing the praises of the Creator. Jouffroy, an unbeliever, one evening on the lake of Yverdun was so overcome with wonder at the spectacle before his eyes that, to the amazement of the rowers, he began singing the *Sanctus*.

And yet, we who believe, we who are accustomed to prayer, are we to pass by all these splendors of creation without thanking God for them? To do so would be to imitate the poor man who, having lost his memory through a shell-burst, gazed haggardly and without recognition at his wife, who stood by his bedside, and played mechanically with the wedding-ring on his finger without any recollection of what it meant or who had given it to him. The poor man was mad. And so are we sometimes.

But not only does God give, with a prodigality and a delicate generosity worthy of Him, but He vouchsafes to make Himself present in everything that He gives us. One of the hymns of the Church calls God *Rerum tenax vigor*, "the force that holds things together." Nothing could be more exact. God is present in everything as the cause of its being.

The books of Holy Writ, while they teem with expressions of praise for the extent of God's power, have little to say of its depth. They enumerate in detail all the creatures that owe their existence to God but, with few exceptions,[38] they place little emphasis on the manner in which God is

[38] See, e.g., Eph. 4:6.

present in each. This latter consideration becomes all the more consoling when we reflect that "God loves His creatures from all eternity. That they should be born on a particular day is new for them; it is not new for God."

Moreover God loves us *closely*. "God's love does not govern us from afar. How can He be far from us, when He is our Creator? In creating, God acts very near to us, for the starting-point of creation is nothing; it gives all. God, then, is present to all things . . . I am not so close to myself as God is, who made me myself."[39] Not only does God make Himself present in everything that He gives; think — to use our inadequate expression — what wonderful activity He displays. Sometimes creation is wrongly conceived; as if God simply cast beings into space and, so to speak, left them to rely upon the mechanism with which He had endowed them, rather like a child who winds his top and watches it spinning on the ground.

This is quite a wrong idea. God is present to all beings, but that presence is not a dead presence but an active one. God penetrates every being by His government; to maintain it in being, He acts. His creative act is not a momentary gesture after which God relapses into inactivity. Conservation is a continuous creation. Those souls,

---

[39] Sertillanges, *L'Amour chrétien*.

therefore, show a deep insight that cultivates devotion to divine providence. God "works" for us incessantly. Long before we were born, He had prepared all that was necessary for us; rather like the mother who, in preparation for the ordination of her son, spends years in embroidering the alb for his first Mass. And on the day when we came into existence, God set Himself even more entirely at our service. There is not one tiniest particle of our existence but we owe it to his untiring goodness and never-ceasing activity.[40]

Hitherto we have spoken of creation in general. Among all the creatures that exist are we ourselves. Let us for a moment consider our greatness. Pascal and other moralists, as well as a great number of spiritual writers, are fond of showing how little we are; but we must not on that account lose sight of all that we really are.

"O my God," wrote Msgr. Gay, "Thy ocean is great, Thy firmament, too, is magnificent; but there is more of Thee in one single human creature than in all these works — much as they tell us of Thy power. This human creature speaks, loves; but neither the heavens nor the sea have

[40] Read the seventh and eighth *Elévations* of Bossuet.

eyes or ears or heart. For man You suffered death to gain his love; You did not suffer death for these mighty waves nor for the sunny skies."

Go up a hill or a mountain one fine evening, and gaze upon the sight before you. All is bathed in an enchanting light. The country cottages stand out in vivid colors. There in the distance is a church steeple, a dome, the sails of a ship. Nearer are the song of birds, the hum of insects playing in the sun; innumerable perfumes fill the air. Above your head is a sky unusually blue, with here and there a wisp of cloud; high up you hear the song of a nightingale. And in the midst of all this loveliness — you!

But what are we precisely? Why do we exist? How did we begin to live? Why do we live? How do we live? What is our life? What does it mean?

"Everything the sun shines on is real, and so are we. Are we destined simply to adorn a corner of the earth for one moment, to warm ourselves in the sun's rays for an instant, to add one to the sum of living beings on this planet, and then to disappear into nowhere?"[41]

Evidently not. Our destiny is more sublime. Poor beings though we are, a great perspective opens out before us. We

---

[41] Faber has some poetic passages on this theme in *The Creator and the Creature*.

did not ask to come into being, because before we were born, we were nothing. This first beginning we owe to the liberality of God alone. And now that we are on this earth, we are henceforth condemned to existence. Wicked men have thought sometimes that when they have finished their task, they may slip out of existence. Vain hope! When once we have entered existence, we cannot leave it. When time received us, we were written on the tablets of immortality. As far on as the imagination can reach, for all eternity we shall remain what we are, simply because we began to be. It is enough to have been born, never to die. Therein surely is greatness indeed.

Think, then, of the greatness of the wonderful gifts within us, although we seldom dream of giving thanks for them. Think of the marvels of our physical structure, of our intellectual and volitional faculties; the limitless extent of the intellect, the nameless riches of our freewill. To think that man's freewill may resist the grace of God; that after sin he may, with the help of grace, have his sin forgiven, and by a momentary act set himself once more in God's favor. One act may shut the gates of hell and open the soul to God!

Our gratitude is sometimes paralyzed by the reflection that all our brethren have received as we have. Because the favor has been granted to all, it loses its value in our eyes. We think of the gifts of God as if they were like the presents we ourselves give to others. When we distribute our goods, the greater the number of recipients, the smaller the share for each. We wrongly imagine that the same thing happens when God gives us our share. It would have been greater, we think, if there had been myself only. This view is quite a mistaken one. God did not first of all make a "pool" of blessings, then a list of beneficiaries, and then distribute them, with the result that each share was reduced according to their number. At one and the same moment, He foresaw each one of us, and the gifts that were destined for all. What my neighbor receives takes away nothing from my share.

If I were the very last of the human race, I would still have my share in the providential plan. God has thought of me. For each one, God has foreseen, disposed, and regulated the whole system and the details of His creation. My history began in the eternal thought of God. Forever God has thought of me, of me, a tiny unit lost in the immensity of the universe, a little dweller upon this insignificant earth, which thinks so much of itself. From all eternity I had my place, and before the world began, God thought of me and arranged everything in the universe for me. From all eternity I have been the object of a definite, sovereign, and immeasurable love. The composition, adornment, and

harmony of the universe were subordinated to my existence, to my appearance upon the earth at a particular hour
on a particular day in a particular year.

And all this is true of each one, of the very least one
among us. What, moreover, shall we say of the incredible
favors that God has bestowed upon each one of us to make
us that real concrete person that each of us is; to make me
myself, the reader of these pages, this creature of flesh and
blood with these individual characteristics? In other words
consider now, not that in which you resemble everybody
else, but what differentiates you from them all. The story
is almost too intimate to write. How can we number the
various favors that God has given us since infancy? Not
only were we born, but we were born in such surround-
ings, of such parents, in such a country, with such health,
of an honest and pure ancestry, with such a degree of intelligence and generosity. And we grew up amid so many
blessings from God, with the affectionate care of our mother,
and preserved from so many dangers. When we came to
the use of reason, think of the examples that God set before us to keep us in the right way.

How few think of giving thanks for all this! We are
ready enough to complain and to protest when one of God's
gifts is lacking; then there are not enough saints in heaven
or prayers in our prayer-books to satisfy our appetite for

prayer. Truly, if we thought of thanking God for all the joys that He gives us, we would not have time to complain. We think of praying when we are in want. Do we think of praying when we are overwhelmed with blessings? The blind man sighs for the light, but the man who sees scarcely ever thanks God for His gift.

We selfishly shut ourselves up in the comfortable enjoyment of God's benefits, and never think of rendering thanks to God our benefactor. Let us imitate the saints and learn to give thanks. Of St. Francis we are told by St. Bonaventure, his first biographer, that "he beheld in fair things Him who is the most fair, and through the traces of Himself that He hath imprinted on His creatures, he everywhere followed on to reach the Beloved, making of all things a ladder for himself whereby he might ascend to lay hold on Him who is the altogether lovely."[42]

[42] *Life of St. Francis*, ch. 9.

Chapter Seven

∞

Gratitude for the Supernatural Life

We purposely confined our attention in the last chapter to the domain of natural creation; and we have seen something of its riches. We must now begin to speak of the far greater riches of the supernatural order.

There are myriads of worlds in the universe; of these the earth is one, a comparatively small one. On this earth, man, although a noble creature, is a tiny atom. For this tiny atom, whom he has made king, God has arranged all things. Msgr. Gay describes the love of God for man by these four epithets. It is an active love, a generous love, an eternal love, a complete love.

But God willed to surpass Himself and to carry His love to even greater lengths. We have seen what man is. God will make him a god: "I have said: you are gods."[43] Not that God will substitute a divine nature for man's human nature; there cannot be two Gods. But the Most High, while leaving man with his human nature and

[43] Cf. Ps. 81:6 (RSV = Ps. 82:6).

therefore with his affinity to nothingness, will grant him such a participation in His own nature that henceforth man will be capable of divine acts, of acts of eternal value. Man will not become God, but he will be "deiform." By his nature he could not know God as God knows Himself, or love God as He loves Himself; henceforth, endowed with supernatural grace, he may aspire to this ineffable destiny. If he is faithful on earth, he is destined after death to see God as God sees Himself, to contemplate Him face-to-face.

"If you have understood the Christian religion aright," wrote the Abbé de Tourville,[44] "it teaches you that God has most lofty designs for man: He intends to raise him up to Himself, to a real participation in the divine nature, yet without removing the infirmities which are the natural condition of his humanity. Could anyone imagine a more extraordinary *tour de force*? Here is man raised from the lowest scale of rational life to the possession of God Himself — and to the possession of God even in this life by the state of grace. This union of what is lowest with what is most divine is the work of an infinite artist."

The fact that, to signify this deification of man, we use the word *grace*, a word which means a *thing*, must not make us forget that sanctifying grace, which renders our

[44] *Piété confiante*.

nature capable of divine acts, involves before all things the presence in us of *a person*, God Himself, who, not naturally but by choice, deigns to make his dwelling in the heart of His creature.

"If any man love me," says Jesus Christ the God-Man (that is, if any man be in the state of grace), "my Father will love him, and we will come and make our dwelling with him."[45]

The Abbé de Tourville, writing to encourage his friend the Abbé Picard, then engaged on his book *La Transcendance de Jesus Christ,* advised him to emphasize what he calls "that sublime discovery: God in us." "It was when I was about your age that I was first struck with this vision of God. I learned from the Church that God is in the soul by grace and that we possess him substantially within us. What joy!"[46] And some pages later he writes, "What a joy it is to think that God is really present within our hearts; for He dwells there as long as we do not commit grave sin. So God accompanies you wherever you are, day and night, and at moments perhaps when no one is thinking of you. It is not merely from without that He accompanies you, but within your very soul, and you can converse and

[45] John 14:23.
[46] *Lumière et Vie.*

talk with Him as much as you like in the depths of your soul without anyone suspecting it. What wonderfully sweet intimacy with God!"

St. Paul of the Cross, the Founder of the Passionists, when asked for advice concerning union with God, suggested this very same thought: "When I think that my soul is the temple of God, that God is within me, how my heart rejoices!" And again on another occasion: "There are some who have a great devotion for visiting holy places and magnificent churches. I am far from blaming them; but I always say that the soul is a great sanctuary, for it is the living temple of God, and the Holy Trinity dwells therein. The most sublime of all devotions is to stay within this temple." To his disciples he constantly recommended, in addition to purity of intention and modesty in their regard: "Make for yourselves an interior tabernacle where you may stay with the Sovereign Good who dwells within you."

If souls but understood the advantages that they might derive from this infinite reality so intimately present to them, how thankful they would be!

I used [wrote Fénélon, addressing himself to God] to assemble in my mind all the marvels of nature in order to form some idea of Thy greatness. I was seeking Thee in all creatures, and I never dreamed of finding Thee in the depths of my heart, where Thou art unceasingly. No, my God; to find Thee, there is no need to dig deep into the earth, no need to cross the ocean, no need to soar to the heavens; Thou art nearer to us than we are to ourselves.

O God, who art so great and yet so familiar with us, raised so high above the heavens and yet so condescending to the lowliness of creatures, so immense and yet enclosed within my heart; so jealous and yet so affable to those who treat Thee with the familiarity of pure love, when will Thine own children learn to know Thee? Who shall give me voice loud enough to reproach the whole world with its blindness and to tell it with authority all that Thou art?

St. Bernard[47] has the most delightful pages on the union with God to which the soul can attain by sanctifying grace, when it devotes all its energies to loving God. Christian marriage is but an analogy, eloquent though distant, of the union of the Word with the soul. St. Bernard celebrates it in a lyrical outburst:

[47] St. Bernard (1090-1153), Abbot of Clairvaux.

Can anything be more desirable than this charity that unites the soul with the Word so familiarly that it dares to voice all its desires to Him? It is the bond of holy marriage. It is more than a bond; it is the fusion of two spirits into one by a sublime union of wills. Nor is there need to fear that disparity of condition will disturb their harmony, for love is no respecter of persons. Love means love and not honor. You honor when you are filled with wonder, fear, and admiration. In one who loves, there is no room for anything but love. What sentiment do you expect to find between two spouses but that of loving and of being loved?

In this case consider, too, that the spouse is Love itself. But you may say, he is honor, too. I have never read anywhere that He is called so. I have read that God is love; I have never read that He is honor or dignity. Not that God disdains honor or respect; He wishes to be feared as Sovereign Lord, honored as Father, and loved as Spouse. But of all these sentiments, love should be the dominant."[48]

---

[48] "Love is indeed a great thing; but there are degrees in love, and the highest is that of husband for wife. In all other affections, there is some element extraneous to love; but the only business of the bride is to love. She is

Gratitude for the Supernatural Life

When, in his exhortations to his monks on the Canticle of Canticles, St. Bernard comes to the passage "*Dilectus meus mihi et ego illi,*" he again thrills with love, and we feel that he is speaking from experience.

What daring! Either it is the soul that presumes beyond measure, or it is God that loves beyond all bounds. Not content with saying, "My beloved is mine," the soul dares to treat with Him on equal terms and in a manner to requite His love. "I am

overflowing with love, and in this is the joy of her spouse; beyond that he wants nothing; love is the essence of their union.

"But does this mean that the soul that pours itself out in love can vie with the torrent of love that flows from God's bosom? The abundance of love between the bride and her spouse is not the same as that between the Creator and the creature. There is all the difference there that is between the spring and him who drinks at the spring. But is the soul to renounce her marriage with the Word because she cannot vie in speed with the giant, in sweetness with honey, in charity with Him who is Love itself? Surely not. If her love is less because she is a creature and therefore less than God, she is not on that account less wholly devoted to her love; and where there is all, nothing is lacking. Hence, to love in this way is to be God's bride; for it is impossible that she should love to such a degree and not be loved in like manner in return. It is in the harmony of two loves that true and perfect marriage consists."

His" is a bold claim to make. The other is no less bold: "My Beloved is mine." It is bolder still to join them both. It is a bold thing to believe that He who governs the world can, as it were, find time to leave the cares of governing the universe to love His creatures, just to satisfy a soul.[49]

Yet it is true. God condescends thus far to His creatures. Natural creation has its wonders; but are not these far greater? God must indeed be God, if He can treat us so royally. What can be more amazing than the indifference, the lack of gratitude, in fact the gross ingratitude of creatures in regard to such benefits?

All these riches we possess already on earth. But to them let us not forget to add, and thank God for, the treasures of glory in heaven, which are their normal outcome and hoped-for fulfillment. If the possession of God in the obscurity of faith is a mystery that calls for unspeakable gratitude, what are we to say of the prospect of possessing God face-to-face?

"Death is indeed a splendid thing," said a certain young man as he was dying. And a plucky little child, as he was

---

[49] *Sermons of St. Bernard*, nos. 3-6.

about to leave this earth, asked his parents not to cry: "I have never been able to understand why people are sorry to see anyone going home to God!"

Lacordaire on his deathbed cried out ecstatically, "Open to me, my God, open to me!" And many souls rejoice in like manner at the approach of death, so lively is their faith.[50]

A young man who was dying of consumption in a Paris hospital said to his mother, "Mother, when I am dead, you must give me my best clothes. You put on your best clothes for your First Communion because it is a great feast-day, but entrance into heaven is a still greater."

In order to be grateful at the prospect of death, we must have a clear understanding of what our divine life

---

[50] St. Elizabeth of Hungary (1207-1231; daughter of King Andreas II of Hungary, niece of St. Hedwig, and widow who became a third-order Franciscan), shortly before she died, turned her face to the wall and sang without moving her lips, as if she had a nightingale in her throat, thus dying in an ecstasy of song. Cardinal Vaughan had two sisters nuns, who died very young. "I cannot say how happy I am," cried one of them in her death agony; and the younger — nineteen years old — a few days before her death, said, "I am surprised that I have the patience to tell you all this, seeing that I have also such glorious news for you — namely, that I may hope within a short time to see my heavenly spouse."

means. Nor is this always enough, since God may allow us to feel that repugnance to death which is natural to us. But it is important to adjust our scale of values and become accustomed in this life to enjoy all that awaits us in the life to come.

Olivier Lefèvre d'Ormesson had learned of the death of one of his sons at the age of forty. After the first moment of sorrow, he said, "If I had true faith in my heart, I should see that this death is really a matter for rejoicing, for it is certain that eternity is happy for those whose death is holy. I have reason to believe that my son is happy in heaven, since he has led a virtuous and Christian life."

One may judge of the virtue of this son by the answer that he made to Bourdaloue, who had reminded him of all the graces he had received from God: "But, Father, you say nothing of the greatest of them all, which is my death; for does not God give me a great grace in withdrawing me from the world at my age at the beginning of a pleasant occupation? I might have had my heart filled with vanities and a thousand desires that might have corrupted me. I regard this grace, Father, as the greatest that God has given me."

To thank God in this way is the privilege of great souls. Let us strive to be of their number.

Chapter Eight

∽

The Incarnation and Redemption

Every evening, we thank God for the graces that He has bestowed upon us. "What thanks shall I give Thee, O my God, for all the benefits that I have received from Thee? Thou hast thought of me from all eternity; Thou hast made me out of nothing; Thou hast given Thy life to redeem me."

In this prayer, we recall first our existence in the eternal thought of God, then our natural existence, and finally the Incarnation and Redemption of the Son of God. But it is the unfortunate effect of our familiarity with these mysteries that they have lost much of their appeal for us. They no longer have the power to penetrate the thick skin of our indifference. Chesterton finely remarks that to reap the full benefit of religious truths, we must always consider them for the first time. Does not the Church make the priest every morning at Mass ask God to renew his youth: to give him ever new eyes and a new heart to discover and fully to appreciate the riches of the altar?

How to Pray Well

The best way to understand the Incarnation and the Redemption is to see them "as something new, with the unaffected astonishment of a child, with the naïve realism and objectivity of innocence." Our seeing them thus will not make them *to be* a reality — they are real already — but it will make them a reality *for us*, something that we have to take into account. We shall thus discover all the wonders involved therein and be in the proper state of mind in regard to them; that is, an attitude of respect, unparalleled admiration, and a gratitude to which we cannot but give expression.

Speaking of creation, we endeavored to give some idea or at least some sensation of the infinite distance that separates God from man. Let us recall this once more. Think of God infinitely and eternally self-sufficing in that "mobile immovability" of which Magdalen de Pazzi[51] speaks, and in the fullness of His being, having no need of creatures; ever identical with Himself and never changing; yet ever in activity and eternally begetting. He is all. Why should He create? And yet a day came when time began; God created.

---

[51] St. Mary Magdalene de Pazzi (1566-1607), Carmelite nun who patiently bore grievous trials of body and spirit.

The Incarnation and Redemption

Think once again that this earth is but one of a myriad of worlds, that man, however noble, is but one of God's creatures and in His sight is as nothing. And for this little scrap of nothing, and sinful nothing at that, God will become man — in the words of St. Paul, will empty himself.[52] It seems a dream. And yet it is reality; it is the wisest act of infinite Wisdom. The Word became flesh. What has become flesh is the Wisdom of the Father, uncreated Intelligence. Jesus, to use the phrase of St. Augustine, is the "Word abridged," as it were, re-edited in a form that we can understand. The Infinite became a babe in swaddling clothes. Heaven descended to a manger.

What I have just written seems to be not only foolish, but blasphemous. Such abasement is impossible; God is God and must ever remain so. How can we speak of a God made man, a God confined for nine months within the womb of a woman, a God lying upon a bed of straw in a stable, a God playing childish games with the children of Nazareth, and later on carrying a yoke on His shoulders for Joseph the carpenter? Impossible.

And yet it is true. The Word became flesh, but without ceasing to be the Word. The Word became like one of us. That man in the Arab *burnous* passing by, a man like

[52] Phil. 2:7.

ourselves, that is He. "Behold the Lamb of God!"[53] He is in very truth a son of men. His village, His parents, His habits, His friends — all these are known. If you approach Him, He will talk to you. "You do not believe? Then come near and listen to me. You can do as those who call themselves my disciples, and come and pass a whole day with me."

What unfathomable truths are these! And yet I do not seem to think so. It seems quite natural to me to associate Jesus with the manger. Natural for a God to be in a manger! If it were not that contact with trivialities had dulled our appreciation of profound truths, our hearts would be singing a constant *Magnificat*. That we are unable to admire such a mystery shows the poverty of our minds Nothing makes one realize the nothingness of man's nature so much as this inability to understand, this cold indifference before the most sublime of all mysteries, before this divinely poetic and loving conception: the great God whom the heavens cannot contain resting upon the lap of His mother; so small that a little girl might carry him in her arms just as she does one of her little brothers when she finds him crying in the cradle.[54]

[53] John 1:29.

[54] St. Augustine says that although he had found the divinity of the Word in Plato, he had failed to find there the humility of His Incarnation (*Confessions*, Bk. 7, ch. 2).

The Incarnation and Redemption

But besides the mystery of the manger, there is also the mystery of the Cross; after the Incarnation, the Redemption. God became man; but He became a man of sorrows. The divine child rested in the arms of His Mother; the man of thirty-three rested upon the arms of the Cross.

Here, again, familiarity with the cross prevents our seeing it. Or perhaps it is that we have never looked at it enough to be able to understand it. There is the cross that is an article of furniture for the drawing-room — would that it adorned every drawing-room! — and there is the Cross that forms the subject of meditation. In other words, the cross may be nothing more for us than a thing; prayer makes it a person: the Crucified. The crucifix may be merely two pieces of wood in the form of a cross with a figure carved upon it more or less artistically, but in any case, rigid and dead; or it may be wood that for us is still drenched with warm blood, and on it a living God who is dying for our salvation.

The imagination, the mind and the heart are, if possible, more amazed at this than at the mystery of the manger. This man, lying prostrate in a fever of agony, moaning and writhing under the olive-trees of Gethsemane, is the Son of God. This man torn with scourges, whom Pilate brings forth on the balcony of the Antonia, His shoulders covered with a purple rag and His brows crowned with thorns, is the Son of God. This condemned man whose arms the executioners are tugging in order to drive nails into His hands, is the Son of God. The executioners raise the Cross slowly as they would a ladder; the body that hangs painfully upon it, supported by ropes that are half soaked with blood, is the body of the Son of God.

Impossible! I cannot believe it! But what is it that the people and the centurions are saying? "Truly this was the Son of God."[55] But you see that this cannot be true. Either you are lying, or else you are grossly mistaken and your blasphemy is worse than the most hateful blasphemies of His executioners.

But what am I saying? It is I who blaspheme. *Lord, Lord have pity on me. It is not that I doubt. No, not for a moment has Your divinity ceased to be invincibly evident to me. This we believe, and so do all those who read these lines.*

Why is it, then, that the Cross means so little in our lives? How is it that the wood of the cross does not fall upon us and crush us? Why do not these beams cast a salutary shadow upon our vain hopes and aspirations? How could a God be crucified for love of us and yet the memory of the Crucified not pursue us ever with its poignant love? How is it that such a love receives so little love in return;

[55] Matt. 27:54.

that even when we are on our knees before the crucifix, the sight of Christ on the Cross helps us so little in our prayer? Could our Savior have done more to win our hearts? Man remains unmindful, indifferent, unloving. And yet it is man, this dull, unheeding man, that God has willed to remember: "What is man that thou art mindful of him?"[56] It has been God's delight to dwell with him: "My delight is to be with the children of men."[57]

May I say to You, O my Lord, that You have mistaken us strangely. We are not what You thought us to be. We are not worth Your sacrificing Yourself for us. Many insult You; the great majority do not know You. And as for the good, You alone know, my Lord, how little they love You, how little gratitude they show. Have pity on them all, O Lord, and upon me, who, for so long, have been ungrateful.

God pardons us; but that does not authorize us to abstain from thanksgiving in the future. At Bonn, a surgeon, surrounded by his pupils, was about to perform an operation on a farm-laborer suffering from cancer. The eminent doctor warned the poor man that, at the very best, he must reconcile himself to the prospect of losing his speech. "If," he said, "you have any desire to express, express it now.

[56] Ps. 8:5 (RSV = Ps. 8:4); Heb. 2:6.
[57] Prov. 8:31.

How to Pray Well

Remember that this is the last word you will utter in your life. After the operation, you will be dumb." Everyone waited expectantly. The peasant bowed his head, and his lips uttered these words: "Praised be Jesus Christ!"

In certain Catholic districts this exclamation is used as a salutation or greeting. One says, "Praised be Jesus Christ!" and the other answers, "Forever." If we but cultivated meditation upon our Savior Jesus Christ, remembering that He delivered Himself up for us to death, even the death of the Cross, then surely the most elementary ideas of gratitude would make us sometimes pronounce this formula. In colleges, seminaries, and convents the well-known but beautiful phrase *Benedicamus Domino* is used for calling in the morning — "Let us bless the Lord"; and the answer is given: *Deo gratias* — "Thanks be to God." If only we would give to these pious usages their full meaning. In certain monasteries — at Carmel, for example — the first words uttered on entering the parlor are *Deo gratias*, and the same expression is often used in other circumstances. We are perhaps not in the environment in which these external practices are used. But we are not for that reason excused from interior thanksgiving.

To be exhaustive, we ought now to enumerate all the graces that come to us by means of the grace of the Redemption; the gift that Jesus has given to us of His Mother; His

The Incarnation and Redemption

sacred Body in the Eucharist; the Church with its organization, its authority, its doctrine, its infallible teaching power, its sacraments, its worship. We cannot review all these graces; we should never finish. It is natural that some individuals feel more drawn to thanksgiving for one benefit rather than for another; such preferences we must respect. Louis Veuillot never tired of thanking God for having given us Mary for our Mother; Newman for having given us the Church to teach us truth; the foundress of the Sisters of Perpetual Adoration for the Eucharist; Mother Thérèse of the Cross for having given us the constant Real Presence in the Host: "I vow," she wrote, "to accept the pains that God pleases to send me in a spirit of thanksgiving for the institution of the adorable Eucharist."

In reality, each of these graces alone is a world of graces. Think of the wonders involved in the changing of bread into the Body of Christ, in the divine maternity of our Lady, in the preservation of the Church in the unity of faith. "All," said Msgr. Baumard, "is included in one dogma, that of God's love for us. All the mysteries of the faith, creation, revelation, the Incarnation, the Redemption, the Eucharist, Holy Communion, derive from this principle; this is the key to all."

We shall never thank God enough for the love with which He has loved us.

How to Pray Well

∞

There remains a word to be said of another form — the most perfect form — of thanksgiving: that is, to thank God, not so much for the benefits He has bestowed upon us, but rather for the riches with which He Himself is infinitely endowed. The *Gloria in excelsis* that we say at Mass is one of the most beautiful of all prayers: "We give Thee thanks, O Lord, for Thy great glory," *gratias agimus tibi, propter magnam gloriam tuam.* "Lord, we thank Thee for being so splendid." The same idea is suggested in the Preface; *Gratias agamus Domino Deo nostro . . . Vere dignum et justum est . . .* "Let us give thanks to God for all that He is: Holy God, Almighty Father" . . .

We need insist no more. Evidently this prayer of thanksgiving approximates very much to the prayer of adoration and praise. We may remit our readers to what has already been said on that subject.

Book Three

∞

The Prayer of Repentance

Chapter Nine

A Sense of Sin

∽

Unfortunately, we are not only receivers of God's bounty; we are often niggardly and worse in making return to God. We fall into sin; we are past masters in playing the part of the Prodigal Son.[58]

Happily for us, the very horror of sin will be our salvation. Man may fall, for he is frail; but, apart from the case of a hardened conscience, he cannot remain long in sin without feeling a sense of shame. And this is often the beginning of repentance. How often in the heat of passion do we not cry out to God, "Give me my portion of the inheritance. I want to enjoy myself." But when the lure of enjoyment is past, when, far from God, we feel the husks under our feet, when low gruntings leave us in no doubt of where we are and the company that we are keeping, then we are filled with shame and sorrow. We had composed ourselves to sleep, we had lost consciousness and a dream held us in thrall, when suddenly we started up. How could

[58] Luke 15:11 ff.

we live in such filth any longer? We felt we must return straightway to the house of God. Sin makes us understand God: the power of God, the goodness of God. To think that a miserable creature such as I could have insulted the Almighty! I who have received so many benefits, have outraged my Master!

It may be debated which is the more ardent: the prayer of souls which have ever remained innocent, or that of souls which have at some time fallen into sin. There must be in the prayer of innocence a virginal perfume most pleasing to God. But is there not a poignant appeal in the gesture of the sinful soul that calls upon God to save him from shipwreck? After enumerating several causes that contribute to the loss of vocations to perfection, Fr. Faber does not hesitate to declare that the principal of these, in his opinion, is "the absence of a constant sorrow aroused by the remembrance of sin." According to him, the principle of progress is not only love, but "the love born of pardon."

However that may be, surely the most terrible punishment for sin is powerlessness to feel horror for sin. To have no understanding of sin; to drink it like water. How could such a one be sorry for his sins? They are no longer hateful in his sight. What a great grace is remorse, the father of repentance! Even when pardon is obtained, remorse does not die; it remains ever as an incentive to prayer. David fell into sin; he allowed passion to carry him to the extent of adultery, to homicide, and to a cruel violation of the bonds of friendship and honor. But when the prophet came and pointed out his sin, David saw clearly once again. Alas, what had he done! Henceforth, his whole life would be a cry for pardon. In psalm after psalm, the penitent poet is confronted with his sin, and he calls out to God, "My sin is ever before me."[59]

But not everyone, thank God, is what people call a great sinner. Nevertheless it should not therefore be concluded that in such a case, the prayer of repentance is not necessary. Everyone has on his conscience some lack of correspondence with grace, hurried prayers, prayers omitted entirely, stifled inspirations and the like, all of which, from the moralist's point of view, would be described as imperfections or venial sins at the most, but which, to a loving soul, ought to appear revolting, if they were fully appreciated. Teresa of Avila confesses that she did not understand the word *venial*. No doubt she knew of the distinction made by theologians between grave and inconsiderable matter. But she intended by this confession to stigmatize negligence in the service of God. No one who

[59] Ps. 50:5 (RSV = Ps. 51:3).

realized — I do not say fully, for on earth that is impossible; but more than commonly realized — what it means to refuse an offer from God, could ever make such a refusal.

But let us be quite clear on this point. There is always the danger, when one speaks of generosity, of disturbing a virtue that is still more necessary — namely, tranquility. We are not speaking here of involuntary failings, of those indeliberate acts, or, at the most, semideliberate faults which are common in the lives even of the best-intentioned. We are speaking only of the fully deliberate act. Hence, if we are to preserve tranquility — and that we must preserve at all costs — it is better not to be preoccupied at all, after the fact, with faults of negligence that are due simply to human frailty, and in which there has not been complete consent. On the other hand, if we wish to advance in holiness, we must consider as of the highest importance every deliberate fault, even though it be in a matter of the slightest detail, once we are sure that God's will is at stake. Many souls make a regrettable confusion in this matter, reproaching themselves for failings in which there has been little or no responsibility. Let these make up their mind definitely never to trouble themselves about what has not been deliberate. But even if it be a matter of the smallest detail, granted that with a clear-sighted conscience you see what God's will is, then let nothing in the world induce you to resist it.

If in such a matter, you have refused to do what God has asked of you, then reproach yourself with your lack of generosity. God has done you the honor of inviting you to make an act of love, and you, with the full knowledge of what you were doing, have refused it! Such refusal, in one who is able to appreciate its full bearing, although it may not always be a sin, yet calls for a sincere act of repentance.[60]

Some Catholics who do not understand the spirit of Catholicism are surprised to see saints, after committing what we would regard as peccadilloes, abasing themselves in repentance that appears out of all proportion to their faults; and this not merely in the case of saints who have formerly been great sinners, such as St. Augustine, Mary Magdalene, or Margaret of Cortona,[61] but also of saints who have lived lives of virginal innocence. "I derived great consolation," wrote St. Teresa, "from the saints whom God

---

[60] It is a sin to disobey God's command; it is an imperfection to refuse to do what He desires of us.

[61] St. Margaret of Cortona (d. 1297), mother who repented of an illicit relationship with a young nobleman when he died suddenly, became a Franciscan tertiary, received visions, and was the instrument of marvelous healings.

has called from lives of sin. It seemed to me that in them I might find succor; if our Lord could pardon them, He might pardon me also. One thing only caused me regret: God had called them only once, and they had remained forever faithful; I had been called by Him so often, and always in vain. This thought caused me great sorrow."[62]

The saints are better judges than we; they know and understand. For them God is love; and a lack of consideration toward God is the most atrocious evil that exists. They are right. Let us be of their school and try to see with their eyes.

[62] *Autobiography*, ch. 9.

Chapter Ten

∞

Belief in God's Mercy

∽

Detestation of sin is not the whole of repentance; or if it is, such repentance is fruitful only if it is accompanied by confidence in God's mercy.

When Judas came to consider the sin he had committed, he was horrified. The purse that he carried scorched him, so that he could not carry it with his fingers. Haggardly he wandered for a while through the sleeping city, and then went to find the high priest. "I have sinned," he cried, "betraying innocent blood."[63] He had a horror of his sin. As in the case of David, "his sin was ever before him." How is it that his repentance was abortive? Peter sinned, too, sinned lamentably; but Peter, as soon as he realized what he had done, did not doubt that his Master would pardon him. It was enough to see Him for a moment in the hall of Caiphas. For him it was a sovereign manifestation of sovereign mercy. Jesus said nothing to Peter, nor Peter to Him; but Peter's look uttered a cry for

[63] Matt. 27:4.

111

mercy, and the look of Jesus was eloquent of pardon; and Peter was saved.

What was lacking to Judas? Detestation of his sin? No. He lacked knowledge of the love of his Master. Judas did not believe in love. All the difference between a great sinner and a great saint may be a simple act of confidence.

A priest in Paris was explaining to the children the treason of the faithless apostle, when one of his pupils held up her hand. "One minute, one minute," said the priest. But the hand was still raised insistently, claiming attention; the child wanted to have her say.

"Well, what is it?" asked the priest impatiently.

"I wanted to say what I would have done if I had been Judas."

"Well, what would you have done?"

"I would have hanged myself too."

"Would you? And you interrupt me simply to tell me that?"

"Yes, but I would have hung myself around the neck of our Lord."

The little one had a good understanding of her divine Master. To detest sin is not enough, unless one makes an act of full confidence in Him who has been offended.

This would seem to be easy enough. Since it is so natural to us to commit sin, our first gesture, it would seem, should be instinctively to throw ourselves at the feet of the person we have offended, to express our repentance and our hope of pardon. Experience, however, proves the contrary.

Too often the sinner's instinctive movement is not toward God but away from Him. God is so pure, and we are guilty. After their sin of disobedience, Adam and Eve, hearing God walking in the garden, hid themselves. Also we fear God's displeasure, and we imagine in a foolish way that God will find us less easily if we "pretend to be dead" and hide from Him. It requires great faith and deep humility, an intimate knowledge of our own resources and of the infinite goodness of God to get the better of this double fear that paralyzes us.

In fact, what those souls need that have fallen momentarily and are daily experiencing their own frailty, is confidence. And in this there are few that know how to strike exactly the right note. For if excessive confidence is a temptation familiar to sinners — "Never fear; God will always pardon you" — excessive distrust is a frequent error in those souls that, in spite of their weakness, desire to serve God: "How can God forgive you such thoughtlessness!"

Such timid souls may find helpful the following words of Julian of Norwich:

God wants us to see His love in everything. This is where we are so blind. Some of us are ready to believe that God is all-powerful and all-wise; but that He is all love they do not realize. And it is this that prevents many of those who love God from making any progress. One begins to detest sin and to make amends; but there is still a paralyzing fear; for some, it is the thought of the sins of their past life; for others, it will be the faults they commit daily as they break their good resolutions. This fear is sometimes taken for humility; in reality it is inertia and foolish blindness. Just as God tenderly forgives us our sins as soon as we have repented of them, so He would have us pardon them too, and not spend time in abasement and paralyzing worry.[64]

Undoubtedly God is justice; He possesses infinitely that attribute which leads Him to claim from His free creature the tribute of His homage, and to punish Him in case of rebellion in proportion to His sin. But if God is justice, He is also mercy, and mercy, too, is infinite. The one is not intended to moderate the other, as we in our feeble way imagine. In God, these two attributes are identified in one

[64] Bl. Julian of Norwich (d. c. 1423; visionary), *Revelations of the Love of God*.

supreme reality. It is better to say, "God is justice, God is mercy" than "God has justice, God has mercy." Since we are able in our minds to oppose one of these attributes to the other — and rightly, up to a certain point — it may be noted that, although they cannot be separated in God, the one may manifest itself more clearly than the other in certain cases.

Thus, during man's life on earth, it is God's mercy that appears predominantly. God can wait; He has the whole of eternity. He bides his time, hoping for the return of the errant sheep. If the sinner persists in going astray and if his wickedness triumphs over God's mercy, then justice must intervene to adjust the balance. God will not be eternally mocked. It is already a great deal to have allowed man to resist His grace. But now this creature has wilfully turned from his last end and has doomed himself to eternal punishment. It is not God who damns him; it is man who damns himself. Man alone is responsible for his everlasting misery.

But in such a case, with what solicitude does not God watch over the prodigal son, until he has sealed his own doom? This would be a subject for everlasting tears of gratitude if the lost soul were capable of them. Even the very menace of hell is a great mercy. For those who, fascinated by the lure of sin, have forgotten how to love God, the fear of eternal punishment may well be the means of a salutary repentance.

But if the prodigal son, however wicked he may have been, for however long he may have strayed far from his father, will but consent to ask for pardon, God can no more punish him. Péguy has described with characteristic originality and force the demands of God's justice and the triumph of His mercy as soon as the sinner asks for pity. God, he says, will judge us as the father judged the prodigal son.[65]

Péguy's favorite idea is that confidence in God has not a sufficiently prominent place in our prayer of repentance:

Why tremble at the thought of God? Do we think He spends His time setting traps for us and enjoying the sight of our falls? Why do we consume ourselves with anxiety? These sins that cause us so much worry, well, we ought not to have committed them; but now it is too late; yesterday is done, let us think of tomorrow. When the pilgrim has walked along a muddy road, before crossing the threshold of the church, he carefully wipes his feet. But once he is in church, he thinks no more of his feet. He has eyes and thought for nothing but the altar where Jesus

[65] *Mystère des Saints Innocents.*

Christ is truly present. It is true that we are sinners; but if we left out of account all sinners, there would be few Christians left. There are three theological virtues. Faith and charity are the two elder sisters, and between them is the young one, hope. The two elder sisters walk in front, busy with the present time. The little one holds the train; she is occupied with the future.

Hope works miracles; it makes new souls of old. "I will arise and go to my father." Hope does not blush to come in search of man even in the shame of sin. No virtue is more active in the heart of man. Hope is like a Little Sister of the Poor who does not mind handling a sick man. It is precisely when the heart is sick with sin and shame that hope opens into bloom. "I will arise and go to my father."

How is it that this spring of Hope perpetually flows, and flows ever young, ever pure, ever fresh? Where does this child draw so much fresh water? Does she create it as she wants it? No: her secret is not a difficult one to understand. If she wanted clear water to make her clear springs, she would never find enough in the whole of creation. But it is of murky water that she makes her springs of pure water, and therefore she will never want for it.

How to Pray Well

This theology of hope, popular, but at the same time sublime, needs especially at the present day to be made familiar to all.

"Have you noticed," writes Durel, "how sad we all are? Take any man of the present generation, and you will not have to seek far below a surface of mockery or indifference to find a spirit of deep melancholy. When we think that one day we shall have to appear before the Judge, we are seized with fright, for it seems impossible that we should be saved. There can be no state more displeasing to God than this, no state more indisposed to His grace, for there is none that is more insulting to His goodness."[66]

[66] *Bulletin des Professeurs Catholiques de l'Université*, April 5, 1913.

Chapter Eleven

౪

The Purpose of Amendment

⚭

Together with sorrow for sin, a sorrow animated by a lively confidence in the divine mercy, the prayer of repentance will be accompanied by a firm resolve to do one's best to please God in future and never to fall again. Nevertheless we are confronted with a future filled with possibilities of sin. Ours is a mixed nature and our actions are a mixture of good and bad; what we offer to God is seldom perfect. Human nature is allied to dust, and we shall do well never to forget it.

Not only are we a mixture of matter and spirit, but we have a fallen nature. God had raised that nature above itself, and through Original Sin we lost the glorious gift of the supernatural. Happily the Word Incarnate intervened to restore to us all that we had lost.

When we say *all*, we must make a distinction. God had given to Adam and Eve three kinds of gifts: natural (body and soul), supernatural (a gratuitous and ineffable participation in the divine life), and finally something between the two, certain preternatural gifts given in order more readily to adapt our natural life to our supernatural life: the threefold immunity from suffering, from death, and — what interests us particularly here — from the rebellion of man's lower powers against his higher, of the senses against the spirit.

Such was man in his original state. Will man redeemed be in exactly the same state during this life? No. Christ, by His redemption, merited that the supernatural should be restored to us. He did not think it opportune to restore to us at the same time the preternatural privileges that had been granted to Adam and Eve, privileges which, although in our gross estimation they would appear to be greater because their effects are more perceptible, are as nothing in comparison with the supernatural properly so called.

Adam and Eve had been made partakers of the divinity, and so shall we. But whereas Adam and Eve were not destined to suffer, we shall suffer; whereas they were not destined to die, we shall die; whereas — and this is the important thing from our point of view — Adam and Eve were not subject to the assaults of concupiscence, we shall be at grips with instincts or evil passions and also with temptations from without. It is a strange but undeniable fact that Christ, although obviously he might have done otherwise, did not choose to grant us these privileges. So much so that He willed Himself to be subject to suffering and to death. Internal temptations of concupiscence He could not suffer — they would have been incompatible with the infinite sanctity of the Son of God — but at least He allowed Himself to be tempted from without by the Devil.

It is clear from this comparison of the state of Adam and Eve with ours that, while both are made partakers of the divine life — and that is the chief thing — our first parents have over us this advantage: that their nature was perfectly balanced, and they never felt the revolt of their lower powers. So perfect were they that the difficulty is in explaining how it was possible for them to sin, seeing that they were immune from concupiscence. As far as we are concerned, these principles make it quite evident why sin is so easy for us. We must be ever on our guard with a firm will to repress our evil inclinations. A purpose of amendment, however firm, an absolution, however complete, does not transform us into angels. We remain human, bearing concupiscence within us. Each one of us, it has been said, is coupled with a monster. If we are not to be torn by the monster that is in us so close to the angel, the angel must watch and pray.

∞

There are many loyal souls striving after perfection that are surprised to find themselves, after periods of constancy, falling again into the faults of the past. "If I fall again into sin," they say, "was my repentance to God not true repentance; was my promise to God not a sincere one? And yet it seems to me that I was sincerely resolved never to sin again."

Doubtless you were sincere, and God knows that you were. But we are not always in the same state of mind. The fact that I sin today does not prove that yesterday my promise to be constant in the service of God was insincere. I may be sincere, but still be weak. We must be zealous for constancy, but let our zeal be untroubled. "It is no wonder," says St. Francis de Sales[67] with his usual common sense, "that infirmity should be infirm, feebleness feeble and misery wretched. We must raise ourselves as much as we can, until God raises us to heaven; as long as we are raising only ourselves, we are not carrying anything much."

Hence, there is no need to be impatient if, in spite of our good resolutions, we succumb to weakness. "All these complaints," writes the encouraging Doctor again, "are made at the bidding of a certain spiritual director whose name is self-love." Doubtless we must exert all our energies to avoid sin, but even in the midst of our sins, let us preserve tranquility of mind.

---

[67] St. Francis de Sales (1567-1622), Bishop of Geneva.

The Purpose of Amendment

Once upon a time at Myans, in the neighborhood of Chambéry, not far from the mountain of Grande-Chartreuse, there was a landslide, and a mountain came crashing down. The ruins were spread over an extensive area and buried six villages. The ground is all dented and cracked, and here and there a bit of rock crops out. But between these rocks, the ground has not been left uncultivated. Step by step, the ground has been regained, and wherever it was possible, vines have been planted, houses erected, and gardens laid out.

So must we do in our lives. Between each one of our sins, we must plant a fruitful peace. Our nature has fallen from its high estate, and the soil is unfruitful. But God does not ask of that soil more than it is able to give. Let us by our efforts make it yield its maximum, and where we cannot get rid of the rocks, let us plant a fruitful vine in the open spaces, and the divine husbandman will reap the fruit.

It will be understood in what spirit we write these last lines. Certain souls live in such an atmosphere of worry. They insist on seeing only their faults; they never will see the good that God allows them to accomplish. To them we would give the advice given by the Abbé de Tourville to one of these tormented souls. "I want you to have the *virtue* of being satisfied with yourself; a satisfaction that arises not from a reflection that you have nothing to desire, but from the thought that one must have a little enjoyment." And he adds, with a wise psychological insight: "Do not be one of those who are, or who appear to be, always annoyed with their imperfections. It is a good thing to be well acquainted with our imperfections, but let us bear them with charity toward our own souls; and let us have the humility to reflect that it is extraordinary that we are not infinitely worse than we are. This, more than anything else, will cheer us, if only we keep returning to the conviction that in ourselves we must be content with little. This is perhaps a side of humility that has not yet occurred to you. It is a good thing to rejoice in one's spiritual poverty, because this poverty is not the final stage, and because, however little we may have, we are millionaires, for the smallest gifts of God are priceless."[68]

Does not this point of view make for serenity of mind? Instead of complaining of being able to do little, let us rejoice at being able to do the little that we can; let us not get out of breath in our quest of perfection. We are too ready to imagine that the sanctity of the saints is for us. We must sanctify ourselves, but in the measure that is intended for us. Never fear; we shall never reach the degree

[68] *Piété confiante*.

of sanctity that God would have us reach; we are too weak for that.

But our degree of virtue is not our neighbor's. Not everything is for everybody. Let us resign ourselves to not being a John of the Cross[69] or a Margaret Mary or a Little Flower. I do not say: let us resign ourselves to not being saints; but let us be saints according to the sanctity that is destined for us, adapted for us. David had no use for the armor of Goliath, having only a sling, which, however, he knew how to use. So let us not be disheartened when we read the lives of the saints, just as, when we pass through the armor-room of a historical museum, we are not unhappy at not being giants, able to wear heavy suits of armor and to wield mighty two-handed swords.

There are some who do nothing but lament and fear at the thought of the future. How will they ever do any good, they ask. An excellent way of preserving one's peace of mind is never to forget that our sanctification is the work of two: our Lord and ourselves. As far as we are concerned, it may well be that we shall fall far short of what is required. But let us not remain with our thoughts fixed upon that reflection. The more we play our part, the more our

[69] St. John of the Cross (1542-1591), Spanish Carmelite mystic, and reformer of the Carmelite Order.

How to Pray Well

Lord will play His. Our Christian destiny is to be other Christs, the "complement" of Christ. If we have failed in our part, then He, our divine "supplement," will have to do His own part and ours too. We have given Him the opportunity of playing to a fuller degree His part of "supplement." God be praised for it!

So, whatever happens — we are speaking always in the supposition of a good soul, and of his conduct in regard to common failings — let your soul be glad. If you are ever constant in God's service, then be glad for your constancy. If you are in some things unfaithful, then still be glad, because you will have given Jesus the opportunity of being "Jesus" all the more.

Thus, a conscience that is wise and well educated is never in the grip of fear. It is humble, constant, generous, peacefully repentant, even heartbroken with sorrow, but always — and this is an indispensable condition for a fruitful spiritual life — *serene*.

Book Four

The Prayer of Petition

Chapter Twelve

The Nature of Petition

∽

There are two current definitions of prayer in general. Sometimes prayer is said to be the raising of the soul to God to render to Him the service that is His due. At other times it is said to be the raising of the soul to God to obtain His help. The great theologian Suarez insists especially on the first aspect of prayer: *ascensus ad Deum*, the raising of oneself to God. St. Thomas discusses the second at greater length: *petitio decentium*, asking for useful blessings. For a complete definition, the two must be united. The first is concerned more with adoration, thanksgiving, and repentance; of these we need say no more. The second has more regard to the prayer of petition, with which precisely we now have to deal.

Let us recall that "petition" takes the fourth place in the hierarchy of prayer. It is not the whole of prayer, nor is it even the principal part of prayer. Let us beware of imagining our relations with God as merely relations of interest: "I need something; God has plenty; let us ask Him for it."

How to Pray Well

St. Francis de Sales has little patience with this narrow outlook on the part of some Christians: "I cannot bear to hear people always talking about merits." Some consider piety as a sort of investment. Such piety is not bad, but it is far from perfect. Everyone knows the story of the gallant captain who, when on a colonial expedition, found himself confronted with an enormous gorilla: "Holy Mother," he prayed, "free me from the company of this ugly baboon, and I promise to go up to Notre Dame de la Garde in a carriage." And as the gorilla still retained its threatening attitude, the captain began to bargain with the Holy Mother: "I'll make it candles instead of lanterns, with four horses, or mules if you prefer . . . Come, make it six white mules, and we'll say no more about it!"

Yet we must beware of exaggeration. We may well understand a St. Teresa objecting to her nuns' being pestered by good people who came to ask prayers for their success in a lawsuit, or in business. The contemplative life has other aims in view! "Christendom is on fire," she said, "wicked heretics want, as it were, to condemn Jesus Christ to death a second time. And would you have us waste time in offering petitions which, if they were granted, would probably only result in shutting another soul out of heaven? No, my sisters, this is no time to approach God on business of so little importance. And were it not for human weakness and for the sake of charity, I would like to let everyone know that it is not in interests such as these that fervent prayer is to be offered in this monastery."

But the fact that there is a hierarchy in the different forms of prayer, and that in this hierarchy the prayer of petition takes the last place, the fact that prayer for success in temporal matters is of a less high order, does not make such prayer worthy of blame. Cassian, it seems to me, was wrong when he wished to interpret the last petitions of the Our Father in a purely spiritual sense; he goes too far when he prescribes abstinence from all temporal petitions: "The Founder of eternity," he says, "wants us to ask for nothing temporal, nothing that passes away. It is an insult to His magnificent generosity to neglect asking for things that last forever, and to prefer asking for transitory and ephemeral things; the baseness of such a prayer will offend rather than propitiate our Judge."[70]

This is an exaggeration, and asks too much of human weakness. Nuns, fathers of the desert, and even fervent Christians have better things to do than to ask for temporal favors, it is true. But it would be wrong to conclude that to ask God for success in an examination, for example, or for the cure of some disease, is sinful. Although this

[70] *Collationes*, IX, *De oratione*, ch. 24.

prayer may not be of a high order, yet it is still an honor paid to the power invoked. Even though in our prayer we are thinking much more of ourselves than of Him, although we ask for a trifle, a very earthly favor, yet God is glad to see us on our knees before Him.

There are some who like enumerating their wants. It does them good, relieves them by giving vent to that instinctive inclination to cry out when one is suffering. God welcomes and in fact invites such requests: "Ask and you shall receive . . . Hitherto you have not asked anything in my name."[71] The Church and the saints also encourage this admirable simplicity. The Curé d'Ars used to give this advice: "Speak to God as a child does to his mother: 'give me a piece of bread, give me your hand, kiss me.' " There are others who, confident in the all-seeing knowledge of Him from whom nothing is hid, are content to speak to His Heart. They do not try to give Him information by explicitly mentioning their wants, for they know it is not necessary; they seek only to appeal to His pity. "Lord, see how wretched I am; Lord, have pity on me. Thou, O Lord, art infinite mercy and goodness, give me all that I need."

Jacques Rivière, when a prisoner of war in Germany, wrote as follows: "This morning when I asked God to

---

[71] Cf. Matt. 7:7; John 16:24.

protect my dear ones, I slyly but lovingly refrained from mentioning them separately; I just handed them to Him in a lump, leaving Him to know who they were, and to disentangle them for Himself."

Others trust themselves entirely to His love, and think they have done enough when they have called His attention to a particular need. Our Lady at Cana gives us a beautiful example of this confidence in God's love: "They have no wine."[72] She does not ask; it is enough to point out the want; she knows that for Jesus to see distress and to give assistance is one and the same thing, especially when His Mother intercedes.

Péguy learned once that his child, staying at Berck with his mother, had fallen ill. He set out on foot from Paris to Chartres, a journey of three days. On his arrival, he made no inquiries, having committed the child unreservedly to the care of our Lady. He was sure that the child would recover; and in fact the child was completely restored to health.

We may ask something for ourselves, or we may ask for others; the situation is not the same in both cases. Our Lord says, "Ask and it shall be given to you, *dabitur vobis*." If you display your own needs to God, the Master has

[72] John 2:3.

given His word to attend to them. But if you plead the cause of another, God is not bound in the same way.

Moreover, if we are to be sure of receiving what we ask, the need must be one that concerns the soul. If we ask favors for the body that God sees to be detrimental to our spiritual interests, He would be cruel to grant them. If someone asks for health and God foresees that this grace will compromise his eternal salvation, we cannot reproach the Most High for refusing it.

If we ask a supernatural grace for another, God has no reason for refusing it, and, without being bound by His word to grant it, He does so, but under conditions we shall later explain.

Elisabeth Leseur used often to pray thus:

My God, by the precious Blood of Jesus, grant me these five graces today: 1) The conversion of a sinner; 2) the conversion of a heretic, an infidel or a Jew; 3) the salvation of someone who is dying in danger of eternal damnation; 4) a vocation to the priesthood or to the religious life; 5) the grace for a new soul to have a greater appreciation of the mystery of the Eucharist.

Is not God himself more desirous of these five graces than Elisabeth, in whom He Himself inspired the petition?

Fr. Faber, in *All for Jesus*, writes:

> If every night before we went to sleep, we begged our dear Lady to offer up to God the Blessed Passion and the Precious Blood of her dear Son for grace to hinder one mortal sin, somewhere in the world, during that night, and then renewed the same offering in the morning for the hours of daylight, surely such an offering, and by such hands, could not fail to win the grace desired; and then each one of us might probably hinder 730 mortal sins every year; and if a thousand of us made these offerings, and persevered in them for twenty years . . . there would be more than fourteen million mortal sins prevented.

Unfortunately it sometimes happens when we pray for another that our prayer meets the obstacle of a hard heart that refuses to repent or to love God. When we pray for another, his freedom has to be taken into account. He is able to resist God's grace and to resist our efforts or our merits. But such efforts, such merits, are never lost; if they do no good to the person for whom we intercede, they are reserved in the treasury of the Communion of Saints, and will help someone in his need when God judges it opportune.

How to Pray Well

Even when God hears the prayer that we offer for another, He may not always answer it in the way we expect. St. Monica asked God that Augustine should not leave her to go to Carthage. God did not hear her prayer. He took Augustine to Carthage, but there he converted him. The prayer of Monica did not prevent his departure from her, but it brought about his return to God. When our requests are impracticable or dangerous, God answers our intention, if He does not grant the request. Many prayers said by adults are like the prayer of the little child who, to obtain the cure of her little friend who was feverish, prayed: "Little St. Thérèse, make her temperature zero, make it zero!"

Why does God want us to pray? He knows all our needs; the life of every creature depends upon the being that it receives from God . . . God knows what a mineral needs for existence, a plant for growth, an animal for its development and reproduction. These do not need to call God's attention to their needs; for the rest, they would be hard put to it to do so! Why, then, does not man follow the universal law? Why must he ask to receive, in fact, ask under pain of not receiving? Does not God know the least of our failings, the innumerable needs that are our only possession?

The Nature of Petition

Doubtless God might have decided to grant us His graces without requiring us to display our needs and ask Him to supply them. But He has judged it more in keeping with His dignity and ours not to act in this way. Many blessings will never be obtained except by prayer.

Man is endowed with intelligence, reason, and freedom. It is not natural for him to receive the gifts of God blindly and passively; he is capable of discovering their beauty, of feeling their need and of desiring their acquisition. Hence, God has willed that by prayer the rational creature should mingle his activity in the harmonious plan of providence.

It is true that prayer puts man in his place as a creature; it is a sign of his weakness and his essential poverty. "When we pray," says St. Augustine, "we are beggars of God's bounty." Nonetheless this poor beggar is a "cog in the wheel of providence."

"Prayer," says E. Hello, "is a confession of poverty, it puts man on his knees. It is a confession that man is poor and blind and needy, a suppliant like the beggar in the Gospel. But it is also a clear indication of man's greatness, for of his prayers account is taken in God's decrees. By prayer, God initiates us into the mystery of the government of the universe; and that moment in which He takes us into His counsels is the moment in which He flings us on our knees before Him. Prayer is at the same time a cry of distress and a hymn of glory."[73]

When the woman of Canaan asked that her daughter might be healed, our Lord seemed at first to repulse her. But when she importuned Him, the Master at last answered her: " 'Be it done to thee as thou wilt.' And her daughter was cured from that hour."[74] When God had decided to destroy Sodom and Gomorrha, and Abraham interceded, angels from above asked him not to intercede any longer, so that the punishment might be carried out.[75] Similarly with Moses.[76] Such is the effect of man's prayer upon God's actions.

> *L'océan a sa masse et l'astre sa splendeur,*
> *L'homme est l'être qui prie, et c'est là sa grandeur.*[77]

Prayer raises man aloft while it casts him on his knees; it puts into his hands a supreme power.

---

[73] *L'homme.*

[74] Matt. 15:28.

[75] Gen. 18:20 ff.

[76] "When God wanted to punish the Jewish people, He said to Moses, 'Pray not to me, for my anger must be kindled against my people.' Moses prayed and God spared His people" (sermon of the Curé d'Ars).

[77] Lamartine.

The Nature of Petition

Here is a sinful will and a child's prayer. The sinner is hardened; all the graces of God have failed before the impregnable wall of his closely guarded soul; the child is ten years old, and the sinner is his father. There had been a sermon on prayer.

"You said," exclaimed the child to the missionary, "that a prayer made with faith will work miracles. I have already prayed much, yet my father is not converted."

"Patience, my child, God will work the miracle."

And every time the child saw him, it was always the same: "The miracle is not worked yet."

Then came the day of his First Communion, and the child was sad.

"Why are you crying?" asked the father.

"Because you will not be at my side at the Communion rail."

"Who told you, child, that I should not be at your side? Come, don't cry, I will go with you."

The miracle was worked. And how often this miracle takes place. A criminal is about to die unreconciled with God, and a child prays; her name is Thérèse of the Infant Jesus, and she asks God to give a clear sign of His sovereign power. The sinner was converted by the prayer of the child Thérèse. Every missionary, every preacher has some similar experience. It is daily history.

How to Pray Well

Not only the fate of individuals but that of communities also depends upon prayer. "Peoples and individuals," writes a convert, afterward a Passionist, George Spencer, "may return to the faith in three ways: by way of miracle, of punishment, or of prayer. May we not hope that God will use the third means to call us back to Him?"

While prayer is a glory for him who prays, it is also a glory for God, to whom the prayer is addressed. Is not a mother happy to receive a request from her child? Is it not an acknowledgment of her goodness, wisdom, and power? So when we pray to God for His graces; by asking a favor, we declare that He is supremely wise, powerful, and good.

Presiding at a distribution of prizes in Paris in the year 1877, Legouvé said, "If I were absolutely forced to choose for a child between learning to pray and learning to read, I should say, let him learn to pray. To pray is to read the most beautiful of all books on the brow of Him from whom all light, all justice, and all goodness flow."

What makes our modern secularizers so reluctant to accept God and their duties to God, Jesus Christ, his doctrine, and His commandments, is a foolish pride — foolish is the only word — with which they are filled. Are not these the words of a madman that Jaurès uttered in the *Chambre des Députés:* "The first thing to hold firmly is that every truth that does not come from within us is a lie;

so much so that if the divine ideal were to render itself visible, if God Himself appeared before the multitudes in palpable form, the first duty of man would be to refuse obedience and to consider him as an equal with whom to discuss, not as a master to whom to submit."

Compare with this folly the words of Hello: "Deal with us, O God, according to Thy nature and mine. Thou art Being; I am nothing. Thou who art God, give as Thou art — infinitely. Thou art all; give to him who is nothing." This is the only proper attitude to adopt toward God.

Chapter Thirteen

∽

The Possibility of Petition

∞

"Happy those who are able to pray . . . The gift of prayer is so great that it is hardly fitting to desire any other. To drink is a small thing; to be thirsty is everything." So speaks a doctor who has made a name for himself in literature. After speaking of the prayer offered by the faithful in church, he explains his own method. "As for me, if I walk up and down, I pray; if I see a bit of sky, I pray; if I see the wonders of nature, I pray. I cannot help praying; I do it instinctively." He had written earlier: "I can find solitude amidst a hundred thousand companions talking; there are certain little songs I know which, if I sing them to myself, surround me with the silence of the desert."[78]

Not all the men of our generation — I mean irreligious men — have the same understanding of prayer as this enlightened philosopher. Some of them, perhaps to excuse themselves from lowering their pride to prayer, deny its right to existence. "Ask anything of God! But

[78] Duhamel, *La possession du monde*.

surely you forget what God is and what you are! Is not God immutable? How can you claim by your prayer to change the plans of the Most High!"

Sully Prud'homme puts these uncompromising words on the lips of "destiny":

> Je n'accepte de toi ni voeux ni sacrifices;
> Homme, n'insulte pas mes lois d'une oraison,
> N'attends de Ines décrets ni faveur ni caprices.

After all, what is man? How can you expect God, if He is really infinite, to trouble about this ridiculous atom immeasurably distant from His infinite greatness? Rousseau took up this sophism and made it familiar to all: "I converse with God," he writes. "I imbue all my faculties with His divine essence; I am touched by His benevolence; I bless Him for his gifts; but I do not pray." When he says that he does not pray, he takes prayer in the narrow sense of the prayer of petition: "I refuse to ask favors." And what reason does he give for refusing to ask God's help?

> What shall I ask of Him? Ask Him to change the course of events for me? To work miracles for my sake? When I ought above all things to love the order established by His wisdom and maintained by His providence, would you have me ask Him to

150

disturb it for my sake? Such a rash desire deserves punishment rather than fulfillment.[79]

As against these futile arguments let us see what divine wisdom and true human wisdom have to say. Let us hear divine wisdom first, and especially its chief mouthpiece, Jesus Christ: "Ask," says our divine Master, "and you shall receive." On another occasion: "Ask. Hitherto you have not asked anything." In the Our Father, which He taught the Apostles, after the earlier aspirations, which concern the glory of the Father, the passages of the second part are all concerned with the needs of man. He congratulates those who have faith in prayer and use it with all humility and confidence; so the lepers, for example, who implore His help: "Lord, Son of David, have mercy on us."[80] Better

[79] J. J. Rousseau: *Perfection de foi du vicaire savoyard*. It is curious to see the same inane criticisms periodically repeated, not merely by poets and dreamers, but by real or supposed philosophers. J. Simon, for example, writes, "The prayer of petition as practiced in systems of positive religion will not stand the test of reason, for reason tells us that the divine perfection is immutable. No effort can deprive God of His immutability or His eternity. The only effect of prayer is to bring us nearer to God by meditation and love." *La religion naturelle*, Pt. 4, ch. 1.

[80] Luke 17:13.

still, he rewards with a miracle those who ask His intervention; thus, the centurion ("Lord, I am not worthy"[81]) and the woman of Canaan ("Lord, have pity on me, for my daughter is sick"[82]). And when the little children crowded around Jesus for a blessing or a caress, and the Apostles, fearing that they were a nuisance to their Master, attempted to drive them away, our Lord blamed the Apostles and encouraged the little petitioners.[83]

The Old Testament is full of prayers of petition. "Lord, guide me; Lord, enlighten me; Lord, show me Thy face, show me the extent of Thy mercies . . ." And often the event proves that the prayers have been heard.

All the psalms that are not prayers of adoration or praise are prayers of petition, litanies of supplication; they constitute the most magnificent eulogy of the prayer of petition.

And does not the Church, the Spouse of Christ, adopt in her liturgy many formulas that are nothing else than prayers of petition? "Lord, come to my aid, make haste to help me." Every priest begins his office by uttering this petition. And is there a prayer in the Mass that is not a

---

[81] Matt. 8:8.
[82] Cf. Matt. 15:22.
[83] Matt. 19:13-14.

prayer of petition? "Lord, pour forth Thy grace . . . Lord, grant me; Lord, give me . . ."

Would our Lord, would the Holy Spirit thus encourage the prayer of petition if it were useless?

For the rest, true human wisdom easily refutes the arguments of the rationalists against the prayer of petition. Jacques Rivière thus answers the objections he heard made around him, or which he himself invented:

> The unbeliever thinks the Christian incredibly foolish and ignorant for believing that he is able of himself to do anything to alter the course of events, to make one thing happen instead of another. The poor man, says the unbeliever, is not content to believe that God arranges events to suit him, but he further thinks that he is able to impel God to produce a particular event of which God perhaps had never even dreamed. Could presumption go further? It is really a refinement of absurdity. The Christian would have us believe that his luck in escaping gun-fire, the success of an enterprise, are the outcome of a pressure that he has exerted upon God; that he has obtained them by constraining or influencing the Divinity. Could anything more grotesque be imagined?

How to Pray Well

Evidently if this were an exact description of the Christian's intention when he asks a grace of God, it would indeed be the height of impertinence. But the attitude of the Christian when he prays is quite different.

The Christian has a confused idea that God is able to change events, and, at the very instant when they are happening, to bring about a sort of revolution in them, in virtue of his sovereign right over every instant of history, regardless of the natural course it may be following. He prays, therefore, not to change the order of events, but to make them fruitful, to show forth in them something of God's almighty power. He asks God to take the event and to show it in its true light, and to set His seal upon it as it happens. At the bottom of his heart, he is ready to accept God's will, whatever it may be. He knows well that God alone sees under what form an event may be made to yield most fruit. Briefly, once you have understood what Providence is, there is no further difficulty in explaining prayer; it is simply an invitation to Providence to exert itself.

Nothing could be more precise. God is not taken unawares by prayer. From all eternity He has decided what grace to give and what prayer will help to obtain it. Man's prayer does not make God change His mind. In God's eternal decree, prayer is one of the elements that have been taken into account. There is no afterthought on God's part, no retouching of His plans. Prayer is one of the elements of a fixed plan, and this is why God suggests to man the idea of praying. If you ask why God condescends to desire man to express his wishes to Him, to become "a cog in the wheel of divine providence," the answer is not far to seek: it is because He loves him.

The other objection is even less serious; how can we believe that God worries about our little affairs? How can we interest the Most High? It would be unworthy of a Being who is infinitely great, infinitely powerful, infinitely perfect.

Do you think God does not know His creatures, or knows so little of them that He takes no interest in them? Such a conception of God would be even more foolish than the idea that it is intended to refute. It reduces itself to this: that God is ignorant of the details of His own work; that God is a creator and conserver of the universe who allows His creation to go on haphazard. Is there a point in the universe that God cannot reach? Is the whole of the universe something greater than He, that He is unable to master it?

How to Pray Well

It is objected that it is incompatible with the majesty of God to occupy Himself with beings so insignificant as we are. But is it not much more incompatible with His majesty *not* to do so?

Or, again, it is said that it is the height of folly and pride to want to establish relations between nothing and the infinite, and to think that in God's eyes we are something. It shows that we have no sense of proportion. But where is the pride? In those who seek their Father's benevolence, or in those who claim to do without it? The expression: "I am too little for God to care for me," ought really to be translated: "I am not a child. Can I not manage my affairs for myself?"

Really there is a snobbish sophistry underlying this mock humility, another form of the fashionable prejudice that to take notice of anything beneath one is to lower oneself. As a matter of fact, to care for little ones, whether it be we who care for the poor and humble, or God who cares for us, is not to lower oneself, it is to love, and therefore to raise oneself, or — in the case of him who cannot raise himself — to show his greatness the more.

A truce, then, to objections. The prayer of petition is not a useless practice, nor is it philosophically impossible. It is normal, justified by strict logic, and, we may add, psychologically sound. To be a creature and to thirst are one and the same thing; and he who is thirsty naturally asks to drink.

Before Madeleine Sémer was converted, her son fell seriously ill. Far from his mother, helpless with pain, and frightened at the prospect of death, he could not repress the cry: "Mother, I was so lonely. If only I could have prayed." The mother's heart was pierced, and later she wrote to her son: "Since I heard you utter that cry of distress: 'If only I could have prayed,' I have desired only one thing: to be able to help you to pray and, with this in view, to pray myself with all my heart." Does not this bring us very near to the true nature of the human heart?

Away, then, with those pretentious ones who think they can rely upon themselves alone, who have not the intelligence to admit the existence of God, nor sufficient paternal feeling to understand that our Lord loves to condescend to His creature. There is no greater help to the understanding of theological problems than a little humble common sense and true philosophy.

Chapter Fourteen

The Efficacy of Petition

∽

"Why are you so moderate in your requests," asked our Lord reproachfully of the Ven. Balthasar Alvarez, "when God is so free with His gifts?" Encouraged by this divine generosity, one of Margaret Mary's confidants, P. Croiset, wrote, "It is a wonder that Christians are not almighty, as it were, seeing that they have so sure and infallible a means of obtaining all that they desire — namely, to ask for it. There is nothing which Christ has promised more solemnly than to hear our prayers." So, too, we may understand the wonder of little Gerard Majella,[84] who, when he was out with his mother and saw men loafing idly in the streets, asked her, "Why don't these men spend their time praying?"

Normally, within the limits specified earlier, prayer is infallible. Anyone who, in a spirit of faith, humility, and confidence, prays for a spiritual favor, useful or necessary for his salvation, may be sure of being answered. If it is a

[84] St. Gerard Majella (1725-1755), Redemptorist lay-brother.

temporal matter, infallibility is not promised to prayer; God reserves to Himself the right to see whether the favor in question will be for the spiritual advantage of the petitioner. If so, then God is not niggardly; He grants it. "To ask is to receive, when you ask true benefits."

"I can truly say," we read in the war-commentary of Montluc, "that at times I have felt such fear in the face of the enemy that my heart and members were trembling with weakness; but after saying my prayers, I swear before God and man that I felt a sudden warmth in my heart and members, so that when I had finished my prayers, I was a different man; I felt no more fear." Many, if they were sincere, could say the same, and give witness to the efficacy of prayer.

In the case of prayer for others, we must again distinguish between spiritual and temporal favors; and even in the case of spiritual favors, the malice of the person for whom we are praying may set an obstacle in the way of God's grace. We need not further discuss these matters with which we have already dealt.

What we must do is to arouse our faith. We have not that unfailing confidence that animated the saints; this is why our prayers are often attended with poor results. See, for example, how certain Joan of Arc was of being heard. In the thick of a battle, she had fallen into a ditch. She asked if her standard, inscribed with the name of Jesus, had yet touched the rampart. "Yes," they said. "Then, enter. The day is ours."

On another occasion, when she had gone apart to pray, her squire came to her in alarm. "What are you doing? You are alone." Pointing to the empty space around her and to the sky, "I have fifty thousand soldiers," she said, adapting to her own situation the words of Christ before His agony. Peter had drawn his sword. "Put up thy sword into its place," said our Lord to him. "Thinkest thou that I cannot ask my Father and He will give me presently more than twelve legions of angels?"[85]

Prayer, then, is equivalent to legions of angels; wherever someone is praying, there invisible weapons are at hand. While Moses invoked God upon the mountain Amalec retreated; when Moses ceased to pray, Amalec advanced. The army was the same in both cases; only, when Moses prayed, Amalec had also against him legions of angels, or as Joan said, fifty thousand soldiers.

It may be asked why, even when God intends to grant us a favor, He makes us repeat our request, often for quite a

<hr>

[85] Matt. 26:52-53.

long time, before acceding to it. Our Lord Himself recommends this repetition, and praises a prayer that is constant and uninterrupted. This is not difficult to understand when one has grasped what is the object of prayer.

The end of prayer, as we have seen, is not to dispose providence, but rather to dispose ourselves in regard to providence. Prayer does not claim to change God, but to change in us what might be an obstacle to God's action. A machine will not work unless everything is in its right place. Now, the place of man is on his knees. If, at any time or in any place, things go badly, it is a sign that man is refusing to pray, refusing to recognize that above him is One before whom right reason and the most elementary humility demand that we should prostrate ourselves. It is by prayer especially that we fulfill our function as creatures. By prayer, we recognize that we are finite, and that if the Almighty does not support the building, our poor strength will strive in vain to keep it from falling into ruins.

But why does God keep us waiting for an answer to our prayers? So that we may better appreciate the gift that He is giving us. When a thing is given as soon as it is asked for, it may lose something in our esteem. We appreciate only what we have striven for. The gifts that we obtain without trouble are regarded as of little consequence. Moreover,

The Efficacy of Petition

God is like a mother who does not give in to her child immediately, simply for the joy of having him ask again. If the child asks, it means that he recognizes the power of her who is to grant. If he asks untiringly, it means that he has an unwavering confidence in her goodness.

"God," says St. Gregory, "wishes to be conquered by a certain importunity." He wants to be besieged with petitions, and He temporizes simply in order to be besieged the more. "Hitherto you have asked nothing," says our Lord reproachfully to His Apostles, as if to say: "Come, be bolder; show your confidence in me, and thus proclaim the greatness of my mercy."

A fourth reason is that this very insistence on our part increases our merits by making us practice the most noble virtues. "If you ask a favor of God," says the Pastor of Hermas, "and God seems to refuse it, do not be discouraged; the delay is intended either to try you, or to enable you to expiate some sin . . . If you cease praying, do not blame God but yourself if you do not receive."

How long must we persevere in prayer to be sure of being heard? Obviously no mathematical limit can be set. But here is a practical rule according to the grace that may be asked in three given sets of circumstances.

How to Pray Well

In asking *temporal favors*, pray until it is quite clear that God does not intend to grant them, at least in the manner in which we want. This indication is useful especially, for example, in the case of illness. Instead of asking for a cure, which may not perhaps be desirable for us, pray rather for resignation, which in any case, because it is a supernatural virtue, is greatly to be desired and will certainly be obtained.

In *temptations*, how long must we persevere in prayer, and what must we ask for? Persevere as long as the temptation lasts. It may be that God is about to give you the victory just at the moment when you cease praying. Ask unceasingly. Prayer is above all things the weapon of the disarmed. Ask for the temptation to be removed; better still — for God may leave the temptation with you in order to try your worth and increase your merits — ask for the grace to resist at all costs without wavering. Such a prayer is certainly in conformity with God's will, and its success is infallible.

There is still a third case: the prayer for *final perseverance*, the grace of a good death. Since this favor is directly and of itself conducive to salvation, it may be asked without any reserve or condition. God's only object in putting us on this earth is to grant us this grace; His intentions, therefore, in this case are at one with ours. To pray unceasingly for salvation is to assure it.

∽

Conclusion

∽

Some souls may be led by these reflections to pray better, that is, to give their prayer a wider scope, to appreciate better the principles on which prayer is based, and to understand more exactly what should be our true relations with God. We venture to hope so, and strong in our confidence in the efficacy of prayer, we ask this grace of our Lord. Every prayer, to obtain its effect, must be made through Him. May this one especially be offered by Him to the Most High.

Raoul Plus, S.J.

(1882–1958)

∞

Raoul Plus was born in Boulogne-sur-Mer, France, where he attended the Jesuit college. In 1899 he entered the Jesuit novitiate in Amiens and was ordained there. Because of laws that persecuted religious orders at that time, Fr. Plus had to leave France in 1901 and did not return from this exile for ten years, during which time he studied literature, philosophy, and theology in Belgium and Holland. He also taught courses in the field of humanities.

At the advent of World War I, Fr. Plus enlisted as a soldier, and subsequently as chaplain, and later was awarded the Croix de Guerre and the Medaille Militaire for his heroism. It was during this time that he began to write, producing his first two books, which were followed by a host of works on various aspects of the spiritual life, and in particular, about the presence of Christ in the soul.

After the war, Fr. Plus taught religion at the Catholic Institute of Arts and Sciences in Lille and became a well-loved spiritual director for the students. During school vacations, he gave retreats for priests and seminarians.

How to Pray Well

In his lifetime, Fr. Plus wrote more than forty books aimed at helping Catholics understand God's loving relationship with the soul. His words consistently stress the vital role of prayer in the spiritual life and seek to show how to live out important spiritual truths. His direct, practical style renders his works invaluable for those seeking to know Christ better and to develop a closer union with Him in their souls.

∽

Sophia Institute Press®

contribution to the address below. We welcome your questions, comments, and suggestions.

For your free catalog, call:
Toll-free: 1-800-888-9344

Sophia Institute Press®
Box 5284
Manchester, NH 03108
www.sophiainstitute.com

Sophia Institute® is a tax-exempt institution
as defined by the Internal Revenue Code,
Section 501(c)(3). Tax I.D. 22-2548708.